W9-CHL-746

F
L57   Leviant, Curt.
            The Yemenite girl.

Temple Israel Library
Minneapolis, Minn.

———

Please sign your full name on the above
card.

Return books promptly to the Library or
Temple Office.

Fines will be charged for overdue books
or for damage or loss of same.

THE
YEMENITE
GIRL

A Novel

by

Curt Leviant

THE BOBBS-MERRILL COMPANY, INC.
New York   Indianapolis

A part of this book has appeared in slightly different form in *The Literary Review*.

Copyright © 1973, 1977 by Curt Leviant

All rights reserved, including the right of reproduction
in whole or in part in any form
Published by the Bobbs-Merrill Company, Inc.
Indianapolis   New York

ISBN 0-672-52263-2
Library of Congress catalog card number 76-11609

Designed by Lou Keach
Manufactured in the United States of America

First printing

This book is
—and has always been—
for
Erika

ONE

From his bedroom high up on Mount Carmel, the ailing Ezra Shultish could see the blue bay of Haifa, its toylike boats bobbing in the water; and, when the humidity broke, the entire curve of land up to Acco and the full length of the Lebanon range to the north. With the boats coming and going, and at night their foghorns blowing and colored lights streaking the darkness, Haifa always gave him a sensation of movement, as if he too, in his bed, were floating off to distant lands.

Shultish was unable to judge whether the new pain in his back was caused by his illness or simply by the weeks in bed. But his head hurt, he knew, from disappointment. During his sabbatical in Israel he had met Yehiel Bar-Nun only four times, all during his first few weeks in the country; he had not seen him for the past three months, although Bar-Nun too lived in Haifa. He missed the old writer. He had Bar-Nun's friendship, his autograph, his picture, his books. He had always wanted his voice, and had dreamed of tape-recording "The Yemenite Girl," one of the master's most imaginative love tales. Shultish recited:

3

I saw the Yemenite girl sun bathing by the sand dunes of Rishon. Not in San'a, not in Haifa or Hebron, but in Rishon I met her. I was not afraid of her because she was swarthy, for the sun had honey-hued her skin. On the contrary, I found myself drawn to her hair, fragrant as wine, and to her eyes that shone gently, like the water at dusk off Rishon, when the westering sun sends blue light waving to Jerusalem.

Whenever Shultish read those allusion-laden words he gave them no special intonation, heard no sounds except the silent music the words created. But soon he would hear them. Spoken to him on tape by the author himself. Henceforth, upon reading his favorite story, he would hear the double music of the words and the voice of their creator.

Shultish was fifty years old, a good round number, a halfway mark—to what? Perhaps to the age of Gershoni, who would soon celebrate his own centennial? An age for sentimental souls, a time for self-evaluation. A full-fledged adult. Yet in Bar-Nun's presence Shultish felt like a child, an adoring youngster ready to do his master's bidding. When he had first approached Bar-Nun's shrubbery-encased house at the crown of the Carmel, Shultish thought he saw Bar-Nun flitting out of the house into his backyard. He entered the arbor, climbed the few steps to the house, and rang the bell. To his surprise, Mrs. Bar-Nun opened the door. On the phone Bar-Nun had told him not to expect anything to eat that evening, since his wife wasn't well. But in reply to Shultish's question Mrs. Bar-Nun said she was feeling very well and directed him to the backyard, where the writer was sitting. Shultish ran to greet him. Bar-Nun rose, held out his hands, and smiled. "Ah, Shultish, *yedidi*. Welcome, welcome. How good it is for brethren to sit together," he quoted from the Psalms and offered Shultish a chair. He liked being called *yedidi*, my friend. But no sooner had Shultish breathed deeply and leaned forward to ask Bar-Nun a question than the old man wrinkled his nose and sniffed up at the air. "It's getting damp," he said, touching his black velvet skullcap.

4

"I think we had better go inside." He began dragging his lounge chair to the house.

"Oh no," Shultish said. "Let me."

"No, no, you're a guest."

"Makes no difference. *Adon* Bar-Nun"—Shultish used the formal mode of address—"you're not going to drag chairs while I'm here."

"Well, you're younger than I," Bar-Nun said and stood aside, watching as Shultish ran back and forth three times with the folding chairs.

Shultish was pleased to help. He's old enough to be my father, he thought. Why should I let him do what I wouldn't let my father do?

"The view is beautiful from your lawn," Shultish hinted when he had carried in his last chair, "but the hedges block the overall view. I hear it's magnificent from your library."

"Come into the house," Bar-Nun said, "and we'll have a glass of cognac and some cookies. We'll sit and talk. Well, what's new? How is your wife?"

Shultish told him. He told him all that was new and all that wasn't, regretting that he hadn't asked directly to see the library on the third floor. Now he would have to wait for another opportunity. From Bar-Nun's library, it was said, one could see, like Moses on Mount Nebo, almost all of Israel. Down across the Sharon plains clear to Tel Aviv, all of Haifa Bay up to Acco, the Lebanese range to the north, and the Jezreel Valley to the Sea of Galilee on the east. Shultish offered to run downtown to the main library for him, or buy him any books he needed; it would be a good way to return to the house and see Bar-Nun again, and perhaps get to his library as well.

Bar-Nun shook his head. "Too busy. Too many people. Too many letters. No work done. If I could only tie up the mailman and pull out my phone," he said. "The phone is not flesh and blood, but the mailman—it would be a pity to distress him. There's only one solution. I tell you, I have to run away from the house."

"Would you like to take a little walk?"

Bar-Nun plucked at his chin. "I don't know. I'm a little tired from being out in the air all afternoon. But I'll tell you what. Come, I'll walk you to the bus. I need a little walk. Doctors say it's good for the heart."

Shultish had hardly begun to talk to him and already it was time to say good-bye. The old man always seemed to elude his grasp. Once, when he called him two weeks before Hanuka, Bar-Nun had said, "You know, I've been thinking about you too, Shultish—not constantly, of course, because I've got other things to think about. But I have thought of you. You know what? Not this week. Hanuka is coming up and I'll have many other visitors, and then I have to be in Jerusalem on the last day of Hanuka. It's a long trip, and I don't like to do it, but when the President of the Land of Israel says, 'Come!' you can't be ungrateful and say no, especially since we've been friends for fifty years. So there really won't be any time to spend with you the way I really want to, face to face, and without interference."

"So you want me to call you after Hanuka?"

"Yes, and have a happy holiday."

Another time, a few months earlier, Shultish had offered to take him for a ride.

"Hello, *Adon* Bar-Nun. This is Shultish, Ezra Shultish, calling."

"Ah, listen, *yedidi,* I wanted to call you yesterday, but I misplaced your number. I had it written down, you know, but I can't find it. How are you? Your wife? Are you busy today?"

"No, I'm free. I'm prepared to come; that is, if it won't disturb you."

"Ah, here's my little book. I just want to make sure this is your number: 46673."

"Exactly."

"All right then, when do you want to come, Shultish?"

"This afternoon?"

"Fine."

"What time is convenient for you, *Adon* Bar-Nun?"

"Let's say five . . . But no, that's already late."

"Yes, perhaps it is. At five Shoshana and I start to prepare supper. How about four?"

"Why at four?" Bar-Nun asked.

"I . . . I don't know. . . . Because . . . because you said five is too late."

"Then let's make it four-thirty."

"Perhaps we can go out for a little ride."

"Where?"

"Wherever you like. Have you seen the full length of Panorama Drive?"

"Yes."

"All right then, any place you choose."

"You know what? It's too late for today."

"Then you'd rather I called you a couple of days in advance?"

"No, no. The same day. But early. I don't like to make plans in advance. Things always come up."

"Then why don't we do it today?" Shultish suggested.

"If today, then right now."

"All right. Fine. Now. Wonderful."

"Is there room for my wife?" Bar-Nun said.

"Of course there is. I'll rent a big car."

"What time is convenient for you?"

"Any time, *Adon* Bar-Nun. Let's see, it's lunchtime now; I suppose you want to rest awhile after lunch."

"Yes . . . of course. That brings us up to four already. No good. . . . You know what? Let's leave it for some other time."

"What?"

"You said before that five is inconvenient," Bar-Nun said. "Your wife and supper."

"Look. I can go anytime. It depends on you."

"You see, Shultish, I don't like to leave the house till five."

"All right then, do you want to go at five?"

"Tsk! No good. Five is too late. You know what? This week we won't make any plans."

"Then you want me to call you before Rosh Hashana?" Shultish said, a slightly hysterical edge in his voice.

7

"No. Not till after the holidays. I have to prepare some stories. In the meantime have a good year and a happy holiday. May you and your family be inscribed for a year of health and happiness."

"You too."

When after repeated phone calls he finally did get to see Bar-Nun, someone was usually there, sharing his private interview. Once Shultish sat out on the lawn with Bar-Nun and began talking about his writing. The old man, his green eyes sparkling slyly, told Shultish it was chilly and moved indoors, Shultish once again carrying all the chairs despite Bar-Nun's halfhearted protestations. They'd had one sip of cognac when the phone rang. "Ah, Gutman, *yedidi,* congratulations on your book. I'm so glad you called; I was just about to call you. . . . Come soon. Without fail. There's something I want to show you. Are you well? I didn't see you at the Israel Prize ceremonies. Beautiful. Beautiful. Grumkin's white hair shone like a halo. Of course he was happy. Waiting seventy-five years for one's first major literary prize is no small matter . . ."

Shultish listened, absorbing, recording: simple furniture, walls in need of paint, books piled on the dining room table.

"You'll have to excuse me, Gutman; someone's ringing the bell and I have to go now."

Bar-Nun returned to the table, his smooth face puckered up in disdain, looking like an old steel engraving. "I tell you, I have to run away from the house. . . . If there's no one at the bell now, there probably will be in a few minutes. In that way future and past combine to make a truth where none existed. Prophecy is a wonderful thing. Try it sometime."

"I have tried it."

Bar-Nun laughed. Shultish saw that his remark had taken the old man by surprise, but Bar-Nun showed no further interest.

"I can tell the color of a man's eyes by his voice," Shultish continued. "See him over the phone. Whether he is tall or short. What he looks like."

Shultish's expectant smile faded.

Bar-Nun sat down, then ran to the kitchen and brought back a plate with two apples. The doorbell rang. "You see? Eat," Bar-

Nun said. "I'll be back in a minute. . . .Who is it?" Bar-Nun said loudly. Shultish thought he was addressing him. Questioned about his prophetic ability, Shultish panicked.

"I don't know," he said weakly.

Footsteps sounded in the hall.

"Ah, Yosef, my dear. Professor Shultish, this is my son-in-law, Yosef." Yosef, a slight, small-faced man with Oriental eyes, gave Bar-Nun a book, then shook hands with Shultish. "Thank you for the book, my dear." Bar-Nun's eyes twinkled and he turned to Shultish. "Look. Yosef brings me a book. It seems like a simple thing, no? But think of the wisdom involved here. I consider him my son, you know. In Latin, son and book and free are designated by the same term, *liber*. In German, *lieber* is dear, beloved; and in Yiddish, *lieber* is rather. *Ach du lieber,* isn't this remarkable? When your daughter marries, it's like getting a free son, liber liber, who brings you a book, liber liber liber. And since he is a dear besides, it's lieber liber liber liber. And one more lieber if you'd rather have him for a son-in-law than anyone else."

Yosef smiled, his Chinese eyes disappearing.

And the book is free too, Shultish did not say.

"And the book is free too. So there's another liber," Yosef said.

Bar-Nun laughed. "The man has a head, even though it's uncovered."

Yosef did not stop smiling. The son-in-law, obviously not observant, did not go through the pretense of covering his head in the old man's presence. Shultish felt uncomfortable—his skullcap felt like a plate on his skull—at giving Bar-Nun and his son-in-law the impression that he was devout.

Bar-Nun sighed. "Too bad we're not eating supper together. Otherwise we could recite the after meals grace in a three-some. . . . Did you say the Afternoon Service, Yosef?"

Yosef's lips did not move, but the electricity of his smile was turned off. Bar-Nun removed from his jacket a little prayerbook no bigger than a pocket calendar and slid it across the table to his son-in-law. Shultish watched the chess game, unable to break the tension with a word. He felt a spring about to snap. Bar-Nun

9

pushed the Siddur closer. Yosef, baited, did not bite. Smiling again, he picked up the little volume, opened it, and said: "Leipzig, 1860. Beautiful print."

"Yosef, did I ever tell you the story of how the blue yarmulke floated across the sea from Smyrna to Eretz Israel? A beautiful story that I haven't written yet. No?"

Shultish's heart began pumping in anticipation.

"Well, never mind. You'll hear it some other time. It takes too long."

Yosef stretched his legs, then casually asked, "How are you today, *abba*? Have you had your afternoon walk yet?"

"Not yet. In fact, I'll take the good professor to his bus stop."

Shultish jumped up.

"Where are you rushing to?" Bar-Nun asked. "We've hardly begun to talk."

"It's time . . . you're busy . . . my wife is waiting."

"Well, a wife should not be kept waiting. . . . I'll get my coat; there's a chill in the air now. The doctors said that a chill is a strain on my heart. God forbid that a man should go out into Haifa's night air without a coat."

He decided to ask the question now, to put it off no longer.

"By the way, *Adon* Bar-Nun, when I come next time, would you mind if I brought my tape recorder? I'd be so grateful to you if you would record 'The Yemenite Girl' so I could play it for my students."

"Well . . . the truth is that reading out loud makes me very tired. I don't like to do it . . . but—"

"Moshe has a copy of it," Yosef said. "So you won't have to exert yourself."

"Yes, yes," Bar-Nun said. "I once recorded it for my son. Go to him. He lives in Haifa, too. He'll gladly let you copy it from him."

Shultish stepped outside. The sky was the color of ripe plums, he noted, an image not of his own invention but drawn from one of Bar-Nun's stories. Shultish had that awful taste in his mouth again: sour disappointment. Like walking away half-hungry from a banquet. But the metaphor was wrong; it was a different sort of appetite, the reaching out for contact with fame. Elusive as a woman. As the dream of the well-tanned naked woman in the pool.

THE YEMENITE GIRL
by Yehiel Bar-Nun

Translated from the Hebrew
by
Ezra Shultish

I saw the Yemenite girl sun bathing by the sand'dunes of Rishon. Not in San'a, not in Haifa or Hebron, but in Rishon I met her. I was not afraid of her because she was swarthy, for the sun had honey-hued her skin. On the contrary, I found myself drawn to her hair, fragrant as wine, and to her eyes that shone gently, like the water at dusk off Rishon, when the westering sun sends blue light waving to Jerusalem.

Shultish gazed out the window. A huge ship, two white funnels like giant gulls, was approaching. He made out three blue stars. The Zim Lines flagship, the *Shalom*. He took a sip of water and closed his eyes. Meeting writers in the flesh always left Shultish frustrated. The temptation to see them was a nasty vice; if indulged in too freely, it brought punishment, as any excessive dissipation did. After most visits to other writers, he ·returned with minor metaphysical bruises. Nevertheless, the devil in him to see, touch, look, hear, sense the total presence of a noted living Hebrew author was difficult to overcome. There was still one famous figure, the oldest living writer in Israel, whom Shultish wanted to visit. If he missed the opportunity now he would never forgive himself. Ninety-eight years old, Asher Gershoni was one of the pillars of modern Hebrew fiction, the seminal figure in any history of nineteenth-century Hebrew literature.

Shultish found Gershoni's name in the national telephone directory—he wasn't famous enough to have an unlisted number like Bar-Nun—and called long distance to Jerusalem.

11

"Hello, may I speak to *Adon* Gershoni?"

"Gershoni."

"Oh, I'm so glad I caught you in, *Adon* Gershoni. This is Ezra Shultish."

"Who?"

"Ezra Shultish. I'd like to ask you if . . . you see, I plan to be in Jerusalem next Tuesday, and I wonder if I could come to . . ."

"Excuse me, I don't hear too well; what did you—?"

"Shultish. Professor Shultish. Perhaps you've heard of me or read my stories. I'd like to interview you—"

"Can you spell your name?"

"E . . . Z . . ."

"C?"

"No. Z."

"E . . . C . . . ?"

"No, Z—X-Y-Z. Last letter of alphabet. R . . . A . . . Ezra."

"Esrog?"

"For an interview on tape. This is long distance. I'm calling from Haifa. The Carmel. All the way from the top."

"You'd better spell your last name . . ."

And so on for twenty-five minutes. The call cost Shultish fourteen dollars. He literally had to spell out *every* word he said. Shultish finally got his appointment for the following Tuesday—it was December, the last day of Hanuka—but Gershoni still didn't know who was calling.

Shultish and his wife took the five fifty-eight morning train from Haifa. He hoped he would meet Bar-Nun—it was the day the old man was supposed to go to Jerusalem—but although Shultish walked from one end of the train to the other, he could not find him. When they arrived in Jerusalem at nine-ten, it was already eighty-seven degrees; a hamsin, hot and dry, had enveloped the mountain capital.

The venerable Gershoni, long forgotten in Israel—most people didn't even know he was still alive—lived in a long gray concrete-box apartment house with eight entrances. Which one to take?

Gershoni's name did not appear on the mailboxes of the first three entrances. At the fourth, Shultish saw a woman in her fifties with a shopping bag coming down the stairs. Shultish asked in ornate Hebrew, "Where is located the place of residence of the renowned Hebrew writer Gershoni?"

"Sprechen sie Deutsch?"

Shultish did, but refused on principle. Here, in Israel, German?

"Do you understand English?" he asked.

The woman shook her head, *"Nein, kein Englisch."*

"Gershoni. Asher Gershoni," Shultish said.

"Ah." She smiled. She walked back up the stairs and beckoned them to follow her. "My Hebrew is poor," she said in Hebrew with a German accent. "Just enough to get along. You must be Herr Esrog from Haifa." She opened a door on the second floor. Before Shultish could utter the words, "Is your father at home?" the woman said, "My husband is getting dressed. The hour is a little early for him. He will soon come out to greet you. Please come into the living room."

They walked through a dark, narrow corridor lined with pictures of Gershoni and various literary figures. There was even one, dated Trieste, 1900, of Gershoni as a mustached young man, standing next to the aged Moritz Mitzenfeld, the legendary scholar born in 1798. How the centuries were rolling by! Mrs. Gershoni opened an opaque glass door and stepped into the living room. Shultish felt his entire being expanding with joy.

"Please be seated," Mrs. Gershoni said. "I was just on my way to get some groceries."

Shultish put his tape recorder on the table and sat down on the sofa. As he sank slowly into the feathers, he noticed greeting cards displayed on the long dresser at the other side of the room. From afar they gave the impression of snow, perhaps wishful thinking for Jerusalem on a hamsin day.

"Pardon," Mrs. Gershoni said, and the glass door closed. Shultish heard her speaking to her husband in German, and he, in his old voice, replied in German.

The German Jews, Shultish thought, and the Hungarians, no

matter how long they lived in Israel—twenty, thirty, forty years—still continued to babble their native tongue. It was the Russians, like Bar-Nun, who by their passion for speaking Hebrew had created a national language. Shultish glanced at his prepared questions. *Adon* Gershoni, with your love of Jewish history and the Land of Israel, you awakened the Jewishness of many youths and influenced them to dream of and come to Israel. Has this dream . . . ? "Ezra, Ezra!" he heard.

Shultish looked at his wife, saw by her face that something was wrong.

"What's the matter, Shoshana?" he whispered.

She shifted her eyes to the dresser.

He stood up to look.

"Christmas cards," he said, sitting down again. "From Europe."

A cuckoo clock sounded the hour; he watched, fascinated, mesmerized by the sounds from the distant mountains of Switzerland, or even farther north. When it ended, another began on another wall; and then a third, a fourth, all a minute apart. Encompassed by cuckoos, surrounded by gongs. Then he saw it too: in a swirl of snow and tinsel, an artificial pine about two feet high, with a golden star at its tapering tip.

"I don't believe it," he whispered.

"It's for her," his wife said. "She's a German."

"Makes no difference. Incredible. In Gershoni's house! His early stories could not be more ironical."

"Only in America," Shoshana joked. "A Hebrew writer with a Christmas tree."

A moment later Gershoni came in, a short, wizened figure, unshaven, wearing an old tweed jacket over his pajama shirt. He smiled broadly, a too-even, clicking, pathetic smile. Shultish had written his name in large block letters on a slip of paper as an introduction. He stood, smiled, shook Gershoni's hand and said clearly, "Professor Ezra Shultish."

Gershoni sat down and Shultish flipped on his tape recorder. He blanked out for a second. What was he doing here? As a warm-up

14

question he had wanted to ask Gershoni how he had celebrated Hanuka, but now he didn't know what to say.

When Shultish loudly asked Gershoni if he was still writing, Gershoni gave him a far-off smile that exuded the fragrance of three or four generations and asked suddenly, "Tell me, why do you want to interview me?"

Shultish had prepared the questions, not the answers. Had the old man, still sharp and astute despite his age, sensed Shultish's discomfort and sought to ride him for it?

Shultish pressed the off button on the side of the mike—he wasn't going to leave *his* replies for posterity—and told Gershoni: "Because I like your work. Because you're a great stylist, one of the giant short-story writers of Hebrew literature. But you don't need me to tell you this. I thought that my students—I teach at the Hebrew Teachers Academy, a college in New York—the students would like to share your views about writers and writing and listen to you reading a page or two of one of your stories."

As Shultish spoke he felt a hot flush run over his cheeks and neck; he knew that he had prepared a trap for himself. With thoughts completely blocked by the tree growing wildly in his mind, he had said the words that should not have been said.

The old man, his head hunched into his shoulders, smiled that far-off smile through his dusty plastic-rimmed glasses—glasses that one would discover while rummaging through a long-dead grandmother's personal possessions. Then he sprang the trap.

"Which of my works do you like?"

"All of them. . . . But, *Adon* Gershoni, I came to ask *you* the questions. My answers aren't really important. It's your answers that—"

"Do not deprecate yourself. Your answers are as important as your questions. . . . Which ones?"

Shultish tried to float out the window. Perhaps his thoughts would clear in the pure air of Jerusalem. Outside, the hills of Jerusalem were slowly revolving like a carousel, breathing in the morning heat. Then he found himself staring at the Christmas tree; he had imagined it much larger. He looked away, embarrassed, afraid he might offend his host by drawing his attention to it. Nothing was real unless strangers noticed.

Shultish absently fingered his jacket, touched, remembered—what a lifesaver!—and pulled out the paperback he wanted Gershoni to autograph and read from.

He was about to say, "The stories here," when Shoshana suddenly said, "My husband translated two of your stories."

Gershoni shifted his gaze to her, as if seeing her for the first time. Oh, that was some thirty years ago in Europe, Shultish didn't say. Just a few years before World War Two. Then, from the wilderness of trees, in the forests of Jerusalem, he narrowed the field, focusing until the titles returned. Yes, Gershoni's last major stories, published in 1898.

"Yes. 'The Roof' and 'Passion.' I liked them so much, I translated them—"

"Were they published?"

"No . . . I just did it . . . for my friends. . . ."

"What did you publish? Do you write too? What have you written lately?"

"Yes, I write, too. . . . Have you read my stories?"

Gershoni stared at a spot above Shultish's head for a moment, then said, "No. I do not read fiction anymore. I don't read post-1905 novelists. Do you have any nonfiction books?"

"Yes, I do. My last book is on . . ." Shultish knew he should stop, but, knowing, he said, ". . . on Bar-Nun's style and word usage."

"Ah, Bar-Nun," Gershoni chanted with a little sarcastic cackle. "Now that he's won the Nobel Prize, everyone writes about him."

"My book was published six months before he got the prize. It came out in New York first and then was published here too. And *then* he got the prize. Have you seen that book?"

"I was writing before Bar-Nun was born. Did you mention anything about my influence on his style?"

Shultish wished he were hard of hearing too. Maybe because hard-of-hearing people like Gershoni think other people are deaf, he'll assume that I'm not answering because I haven't heard the question and then be ashamed to repeat it.

16

"That should make an interesting chapter, my influence on Bar-Nun. How did you handle it?"

"Well, you see, I didn't go into influence. I just analyzed word usage, changes in vocabulary. But how about you? Are you still writing?"

"Why didn't I get the Nobel Prize?" Gershoni turned to Shultish's wife and gave her a broad, mechanical smile, like the fleeting smile of a baby with gas. "I published more books than he, and my style was more innovative and influential than his. Everyone imitates me. No one imitates him. Why did *he* get the Nobel Prize?"

Why was it snowing? Snowflakes everywhere clouding his vision. Because, Shultish thought. It never snowed on a hamsin. "Because," he said in Hebrew, struggling through the blinding white light. "Because," he shouted in English, "the Nobel Prize is given to living writers and you've been dead for over sixty years!"

"I don't understand English," Gershoni said.

"Ezra!" Shoshana cautioned.

Because, Shultish restrained himself, your stories are so dull it's a miracle they were issued here in paperback. Who reads them?

Shultish wondered how he could leave with grace. He had invaded a strange domain, gone back in time and found the calendar jumbled. A cuckoo began again. Strange, no more than twenty minutes had passed. He looked for the sea. He missed Haifa's blue bay with floating toy boats and the calming sensation of tides cradling the coast. Of course there was no sea in Jerusalem. But from the Mount of Olives one could see the northern tongue of the Dead Sea, inert and hazy in the distance, and from Mount Herzl, on a ringing cloudless day, the Mediterranean between a ridge of hills. But Gershoni's windows faced south, where terraced hills blended in a conical swirl.

Shultish raced through his questions, skipping most. Every time he turned his head the Christmas tree swished into his vision, blurring, expanding into a forest. He hardly let the old man reply, choosing to interpret hesitation not as reflection but as stubborn silence, and moved swiftly to the next question. At the end he asked Gershoni to autograph his book ("Something to give your children, hah?" "We have no children," Shultish's wife said, "but we'll leave it to our nephew'') and to read a little story into the microphone. Then Shultish rushed out of the house. The noonday heat of the hamsin had settled like a bedspread over Jerusalem.

I saw her first from the sand dunes as I sat by the green dune grass. She sat at the foot of the hill, where the white sand was so soft that the foot sank in deep with each step, and one felt like a primordial creature slogging languidly through the mud, lifting one leg and then another, on the way to the sea. She played with the sand, letting it run through her fingers as sand runs through an hourglass. She watched the rilling white sand; I watched her sun-tanned fingers.

A sparrow fluttered against the window screen, clawing it. Shultish sat up in bed, listening to the rasping sound, and watched the bird until it flew away. He looked at the phone and wondered if Shoshana would call when she had finished recording Bar-Nun's story. Poor woman, not only did she have a sick husband to tend to, but now her widowed sister in Lugano had fallen ill. He vowed to send her to Switzerland once the doctor gave his permission. In his thoughts Shultish urged Shoshana home, placed her on the bus, and sped it through a miraculous series of green lights until the key turning in the door told him she was back. Without her he felt the discomfort of his illness more intensely. Can disappointment bring on what I've got? Shultish wondered. Or a man's words? Aren't the physical and the metaphysical connected? The nerves and body one? He stretched his legs and turned to the side and saw Gershoni on the window screen. What Jew doesn't even offer a glass of water when strangers come into his house during a hamsin? You're not the only one who writes short stories, Gershoni. I didn't notice you answering so quickly when I asked if you'd read *my* book. Measure for measure, Father Time. Divine justice. And it wasn't for you that I devoted four years of my life to a full-length work—can you hear me from Haifa?—but for Yehiel Bar-Nun. Yes. I wrote the book before the Nobel Prize. I wrote the book and *then* he got the prize.

Shultish had tried to emulate Bar-Nun's style in his own early Hebrew fiction, then had turned to English translations of the master's stories. But only two or three were published, in tiny magazines. When Shultish took stock of himself, he realized he had a name but not a big name in Hebrew literature. It was a joke, anyway, wasn't it, Hebrew writing in America? Who did the American Hebrew writer write for? A handful of other writers. Then Shultish tried writing *about* Bar-Nun, but discovered that though his feelings were intense, his critical vocabulary was limited; he felt he was reaching out for something beyond his ken. Finally, he had decided to study Bar-Nun's language, analyzing word changes and phrases from first through third editions, from periodical to book versions.

Shultish had begun the entire project with tongue in cheek, fully realizing the distinction between nitpicking or ant hunting and scholarship. He hadn't had much confidence in his work in its initial stages, and had laughed at the put-on—a word he had recently learned from the *New York Times*—he was planning for his colleagues. But gradually, as the work proceeded, the joke turned solemn; as the pile of pages grew, Shultish began to believe in his research. He worked seriously, slowly, never bluffing. He could not compromise with the ethics of his profession. To his surprise, the work was published and even made an impression. It proved there were other pedants around

When Shultish had finished his book, a certain youthful excitement soughed through him; he would end with a grand summary of his findings. But when he tried to produce the conclusion that would magically unravel Bar-Nun's genius with words, Shultish found that the joke was on him: he had nothing to say.

Shultish's nephew, the mathematician, didn't have to worry. He didn't deal with words. What, one might naïvely ask, could be simpler than words? Never mind—words bore problems. Each word bore a caravan of associations, interpretations. A sentence, geometrically so. A paragraph, story, novel—God, how the head reeled! But a number was a number. For his nephew a word did not radiate meanings like a dead star blazing long after its demise.

For him seven was the digit separating six and eight; the square root of forty-nine. But seven for a writer—oh, the meanings behind it! Seven, with its mythic and Torah associations, seven in Sabbath, the biblical image, the Seventh Commandment. Numbers were cold and temperate. Precision without passion. Sending no chills of guilt or pleasure down one's spine. His nephew's knowledge was boxed, honed, controlled into miniaturized capacitors. Orderly, from one to ten, and then, predictably, onward.

The uncle, true, is the uncle of the nephew, yet it was Shultish who had imitated mathematical precision without passion. The lists of word changes were lifeless—perfect antithesis to Bar-Nun's works. There was no way out. Shultish's conclusion would have to repeat all his previous chapters. Word for word. He had dreamed that after rereading his manuscript some profound truth would emerge; he waited for a burst of something, an academic orgasm, the joyous culmination of years of scholarly onanism. But what was he left with? Information for the general reader and scholar that Bar-Nun had used such-and-such words in the second edition as compared with such-and-such in the first. Here the spelling of "tobacco" had an Aramaic nuance, whereas in the final, third edition, Bar-Nun was already using the modern Hebrew spelling. The little secrets that Shultish had kept to himself for four long years would now be public knowledge. *Style and Word Usage in the Fiction of Yehiel Bar-Nun.*

The sour, uncomfortable feeling in his stomach returned. He drank another glass of water. Where was his wife? Why wasn't she back yet? It was five-thirty already. Had there been another terrorist attack? Israel radio stations did not interrupt their programming for news flashes, and the next scheduled report was not till six. Perhaps she was—He pictured his wife. Now she appeared as one. In his dreams—he had been having strange dreams during his illness—his wife had been two women, equally loved, but if he went to one he was guilty of betraying the other, his wife. And then there was the other dream, the naked woman in the pool.

Ah, Mrs. Shultish, what a pleasure, come right in. My father-in-law has often spoken of your husband. Don't tell me you came all the way here just for one little story? We have many stories on tape, and, you know what, since your husband is a connoisseur of Bar-Nun's works, I'll let you record one that hasn't even been published yet. Absolutely precious!

How easy it had been. Bar-Nun's son was not at home, but Shultish had spoken on the phone to the grandson, explaining that since he was ill his wife would come instead. "All right. You can come tomorrow at four-thirty," the lad said.

Shultish listened carefully for suspicious sounds. No, there were no fire engines, police sirens, or ambulances going through the streets. Nothing untoward had happened in the vicinity. Outside the children were playing, stealing time from their books. Shultish read; others had fun outside. And down below, in the port, ships were always coming and going, wafting the excitement of travel up to him. Children ran in the fields, playing soccer; girls skipped rope to rhymes of their own invention; and he daydreamed he was floating on a rubber raft in some sunny tranquil lagoon, watching date palms and shifting dunes. "Take a book in hand!" was the traditional cry of the Jewish household, and thousands of youngsters obeyed, becoming servants of culture. But whom did it serve, culture? Whom did *he* serve? Did all his colleagues carry in their hearts the bitter secret of their own uselessness, hoodwinked by their students' duplicitous praise? In public they made a big to-do about the value of their scholarship; but at night, just before they fell asleep, when thoughts were clearest and everyone wrestled with his own fear, when in the silence of his soul man faced himself with eidetic precision, they knew—didn't they know?—that all their efforts were in vain; that their words, like dry incantation, as dead as pagan rites, were repeated monotonously, and that no one paid attention to them except the few scholars whose livelihood depended on their paying attention to their colleagues' work.

Soon he would have that Yemenite girl; secondhand of course, a copy of a copy of Bar-Nun's voice, not recorded especially for him; but nevertheless the master's voice. That copy of a tape was, in a way, symbolic of all his efforts. It's not what one fails at that's so pathetic; it's what one could have done but didn't try to do. But at least Shultish had made the attempt, even if he'd had only minor success with his own Hebrew fiction: two collections published reluctantly, at his own expense, in New York—who else would publish Hebrew, or even Yiddish, stories in America, if not the author himself?—and various stories in the two remaining American Hebrew periodicals. A latecomer to the English language, he could not sufficiently master the intricacies of English style to translate well; to continue with the German translations he had begun decades ago was ludicrous. Still, he had published many articles about the nineteenth-century Hebrew European periodicals, to which he had devoted half a lifetime. Perhaps their flowery, artificial language had seeped into his creative bones and stultified his own Hebrew style. A scholar at the expense of art. To copiers the copies of copies go. The rich receive fine presents, poor relatives a token gift. The rich in spirit gathered firstfruits, mediocrities the gleanings.

Shultish understood Bar-Nun—better than anyone else did. Because he, too, was a writer first, a creator. He knew Bar-Nun's lines; the words between the lines. But there was a reading on an even higher level. Good reading is knowing how to read between the lines; ideal reading, he supposed, dispensed with the lines and left only the between. Shultish understood every gesture, every twinkle in Bar-Nun's eye. He knew when Bar-Nun was going to tell a joke because he knew to watch for the crinkle in his grass-green eyes, the tilt of head toward the listener to catch his attention.

But understanding Bar-Nun was not enough. In his dreams, in the plane of existence before sleep, Shultish had another career: composer. Without notes, he scored symphonies and string quartets, but when he woke he could not remember a tune, a note. The same with writing about Bar-Nun. He knew all he had to know— but the organized form was forgotten. Not there.

The trouble was exquisite taste, limited means. His education had prepared him to be a sensitive instrument, not a sensitive player. He was like a quill waiting to be lifted, a violin ready for the bow. One could not very well play oneself. It was against the rules of Art.

Thinking of art gave Shultish a hollowed-out, uncomfortable feeling. There was nothing to reach for or aspire to. Who was it who said that a scholar's life was paddling up shit creek with the academic fleet, from scholarship and fellowship to assistantship and professorship? Was it Kaften at the party in honor of Shultish's book? That party was the highlight of his career. Everyone in Hebrew culture was there. What sort of party it would have been had the book been published after the Nobel Prize he could only imagine. Of course it was Kaften. Because it was he who had made that joke about asking for an increment and getting excrement in reply, prompting his move from Ohio to Connecticut.

David Kaften, a young assistant professor of Hebrew literature from Connecticut, was no older than Shultish's twenty-six-year-old nephew. This had astonished Shultish when he first met him at his party. Shultish had seen Kaften's articles and two books and thought he was at least forty. Everyone old and young was calling him David. Since Shultish had never gotten a Ph.D., he made it a point to be introduced as, and called by his students, *Professor* Shultish. He always felt a bit awkward in the presence of these bright young men, as though standing on one moral leg, afraid he'd be thrown off balance by their élan. But when it came to Hebrew, Shultish wasn't ashamed of conversing even with the master Bar-Nun himself, and was secretly pleased that when he spoke Hebrew to these young scholars—infected by their stay in Israel, they spiked their conversations with slang, neologisms, and inaccurate grammatical forms—they quickly switched to English.

Kaften had written a brilliant article on Bar-Nun, "Conscious and Unconscious Symbolic Function in the Stories of Yehiel Bar-Nun." Shultish found it difficult reading. Kaften drew upon psychoanalysis, folklore, comparative literature, Greek myths, and existentialism. Shultish's head spun. It was something he had wanted to do—penetrate the heart of Bar-Nun—but had been unable to. He was stuck in the quagmire of forgotten nineteenth-century texts and periodicals. Yet it was he who had long ago sensed the genius of Bar-Nun, even before Kaften was born.

"Glad to have met you in person, Professor Shultish," Kaften said. "Until I read your big book I hadn't thought of you as a Bar-Nun scholar. The name Shultish conjured up in my mind a writer of short stories—"

"You've read—"

"Of course, and enjoyed most recently 'The Lake,' in *Ha-Shavua*, and your fine studies on nineteenth-century Haskalah literature. The only surprise is that no one thought of doing a book of this type before. . . . Have you ever met Bar-Nun in person?"

"Years ago in Vienna. When I was a youngster. I hope to see him again next year during my sabbatical. Have *you* ever met him?"

"I saw him last summer. A complex, tricky old man, but he's really the best, Bar-Nun."

Everyone laughed, including Shultish.

Shimshovitz, the host of the party, the dean of Hebrew writers in America, approached, smiling, and drew him aside. "Ah, finally got hold of you, Professor Shultish. I've been trying to corner you all evening. I want to ask your—"

"Bar-Nun," Kaften said behind him to a group of people.

"—advice about some adult education courses."

Shultish shut out what the man was saying,

"You see, the problem is—"

and eavesdropped on Kaften instead.

"The impact of the unconscious forces is complex and subtle in Bar-Nun. Thus his women are a series of disguises, hiding neurotic symptoms. All the traditional interpretations of his love stories that are floating around—for instance, of 'The Yemenite Girl'—are absolute rubbish, kosher-pure rabbinic blah-blah. I don't mean to deny multilevel symbolism altogether, but the symbolic process always represents a condensation of conscious and unconscious symbolic values, easily found in Bar-Nun's work. Freud on Da Vinci and Dostoevski are fascinating from this point of view. Also

24

Ghiselin's symposium on the creative process. And we always have to keep in mind Bar-Nun's reading of European literature and his vast knowledge of psychoanalytic theory, and Western myths, knowledge of all of which he constantly denies. . . . I don't know where he gets the time to do all that reading. . . . If I were a rich bastard—which he isn't; he lives quite simply—I'd spend my time reading everything that was ever written too."

And that was another thing Shultish couldn't bring himself to do—to be vulgar, American, especially in company. Where he came from people were polite; ethical stature was measured by words and deportment. Hebrew had no curse words. But this new American-born, -bred, and -educated generation was different. Since they didn't consider Hebrew their only world, they could be devoted to their chosen career and at the same time make jokes, as Kaften did, about academic life. These younger fellows studied Hebrew literature along with American and English literature, Judaica along with comparative literature, history, and folklore. They saw the strength in the interplay of cultures and saw nothing in a vacuum. They continually plumbed the core of artistic creation, which Shultish too had once done. But not by writing.

He had long regretted not getting a rounded education. He knew world literature only by intensive reading, like the famous nineteenth-century autodidacts. When the Hebrew Teachers Academy in Manhattan hired him as a young, beginning Hebrew-language instructor shortly after his arrival in the United States, one hadn't needed a Ph.D.; in those days knowledge sufficed. He was in his mid-twenties, fresh from Lemberg's famous Hebrew academies. And a published writer, too, making his name in Hebrew fiction. But nowadays the only criterion was the union card.

What had he accomplished? Maybe for himself little. After all, a man never goes as far as his dreams of himself. But his students respected his teaching, his knowledge, his stories. Years after their graduation they were still writing him letters. And when Bar-Nun won the Nobel Prize it was he whom the *New York Times* had called. Yes, no one else but Ezra Shultish. They asked him for comments, and he was quoted as being "an authority on the style of Yehiel Bar-Nun." True, it was only two lines, but no one else was quoted on style. And that said something, didn't it? And his name just barely made page one. " 'The master stylist of twentieth-century Hebrew literature,' says Ezra Shultish, an authority on the style of Yehiel Bar-Nun." Ezra Shul- made it on page one. The "tish" part, unfortunately, was continued on page nine. But he was lucky. In spite of the scores of typographical errors that one could find daily in the *Times,* his name was spelled correctly. They could have substituted a "p" for the "t" and then he couldn't have shown his face at the school. But what a tumult there was that morning in the office, in the classrooms, in the halls. All one heard was Shultish, *New York Times,* page one, and Bar-Nun. All day long people were congratulating him as if he had won the prize, or at least as if he were the one responsible for Bar-Nun's winning it. Even Shimshovitz, that humorless man, offered a smile and said, "You lost your tish in the *Times.*" And the Yiddish papers, which had never known of Bar-Nun's existence, quoted the *Times* piece, as usual, two days later. Once the *Times* had put its holy stamp on it, the *Day* and the *Morning-Journal* and the *Forward* considered it kosher too. It was a surprise to Shultish that all the New York Hebraists read the *New York Times.* That day everyone carried a copy folded into his jacket pocket.

But was that his high mark? How far can a Hebrew writer in America go? As far as Jerusalem. Exported at retirement to teach in Israel, where his accent, and his accent on correct grammar, would be ridiculed. Of the ones who remained behind, some chose translation—if they could write English. To be close to fame. To snuggle next to a famous name. Maybe Kaften could give a reason for it. Those Ph.D.s whose God was Freud or Jung always had a textbook answer. For Shultish's writing a book about Bar-Nun's style they would say: With Shultish it's an obvious case of idol worship. Not famous himself, he had to touch the famous. Unable to write, he wrote about.

At the party, people swirled about him. A face a minute. Yet if there was a circle of conversation proceeding without him, he felt jealous. One group was laughing at the Israelis' habit of changing

European Jewish names to pure Hebrew names. Shultish, he thought; now there was a Jewish name. Not Hebrew, but Yiddish. *Shul* meant synagogue, and *tish* meant table. He heard his colleague Gotthelf saying:

"The longer the original name the shorter the new one. Remember Yankel Dombroshovsky? He became Yud Dov. Silbermesser was reborn as Gal. And then there's Bar-gad, Az-yad, Dan Hor . . ."

"And Paz Gaz," Shultish interjected.

Everyone roared.

Later, Shimshovitz tugged at Shultish's sleeve and whispered, "Who is Paz Gaz? I've never heard of him. One of these modernist poets?"

"You've never been to Israel, Shimshovitz?"

"Maybe next year."

"It's the Israel Gas Company. That's why they were laughing."

"And anyway, my wife has an electric kitchen," Shimshovitz said.

Shultish held back his laugh. He couldn't tell whether the old man was joking. That was the trouble with these Jewish wits who outwit one another. Their humor was so subtle one couldn't tell whether it spoke innocence or guile. The remark deserved a comeback. But since Shimshovitz was the host of the party— Shultish recalled the glow of pleasure on Shoshana's face when in his brief speech of thanks he had singled out his wife for her help and encouragement—he decided to say only: "Dan Hor used to be Horwitz. When he changed his name people said he lost his wits in Israel."

"That's an old *vitz*, Shultish." Shimshovitz laughed. "A joke with a long beard."

"He's really the best, Bar-Nun." Only later, at night in bed, did Shultish realize it was a play on words. Kaften had pronounced the writer's name the way Americans did, Bar-None, instead of the Hebrew Bar-Noon, which of course would have killed the pun. Or poon. Shultish laughed. Now there were many things Shultish wanted to tell Kaften. Things he had learned since he had seen him last. Things that Bar-Nun had told him. But he lay in bed, sick in

Haifa, eyeless in Gaza, and Kaften was seven thousand miles away.

Kaften had caught one of the rays of Bar-Nun's brilliance, but Shultish had once, for one fleeting moment, held the sun in his hands. Years ago, after a hard day's work (he had twice ridden the rush-hour subways back and forth from Manhattan to the Bronx), he had taken a subway back to midtown New York to hear a program of chamber music by Beethoven and Schubert. He loved Beethoven, but the final selection, Schubert's Trout Quintet, seduced him. From his first-row balcony seat, he was aware of the light onstage, the huge space of faintly perfumed air beneath him, and the music, the notes, dying in succession. He followed the themes, felt increasingly tired, and soon dozed off—but it was the sweetest, purest sleep he had ever had. As his eyes closed, everything blended in a blissful state of suspended animation where musical trouts floated in celestial waters. He shut out thoughts, feelings, sensations; heard only music with some extra-perceptive inner ear. Suddenly he knew—was it light or sound, the mind expanding?—he encompassed the secret of Schubert's art; he comprehended directly, now without the medium of music, what Schubert was doing—and just as he approached the ultimate secret, floating, penetrating the mystery of art, he woke. Everything evaporated like a smear of alcohol on a blackboard, drying the very moment it was wet.

I saw her nostrils, curved and chiseled in perfection—that cut of pride and daring—and then her well-formed mouth and eyes that spoke an ancient language I understood so well. But I did not stop there, for one's eyes become intoxicated with a beautiful thing, desiring more. From looking at her face and fingers, I looked at her hands. From looking at her hands, I moved to her arms and shoulders and body. As I gazed at her I thought of honey, the honey and milk that is the essence of Israel.

The other dream was this: A young, well-tanned girl, twenty or twenty-two, was doing the backstroke in a seaside pool, completely naked. Every time she lifted her hands her breasts surged up and the cold red nipples surfaced. Her waist was like the pinch in the letter *Aleph,* and her breasts could have filled the cup of his hands to overflowing. In daydreams he just watched; night dreams provided fulfillment, gave fantasies license. At night she beckoned and he dived after her, doing the breast stroke in the European fashion. But in the middle of the pool a thin mesh curtain he could not penetrate blocked his way; he dived deeper, but it extended to the tile bottom. Was the pool that day like a *shul* divided into men's and women's sections?

Every day the Yemenite girl bathed in the sand, the sun, the sea. I too came daily, for there is nothing in the world like the sand of Rishon and the water of the Mediterranean, which is cool even on the hottest day. He who has not bathed in the blue waves off the dunes of Rishon has never bathed in beauty.

When he first visited Bar-Nun, Shultish had been only eighteen and Bar-Nun was already an established writer of fifty. Before entering, Shultish composed a little speech in the Bar-Nun style, announcing himself as a lover of his works who wanted to thank the writer for enriching his life and that of Hebrew literature. Then he knocked at the door of the Vienna apartment that in the late twenties and early thirties was already a center of Hebrew culture. Bar-Nun greeted him with his hand on his heart and a little bow of his head, which made Shultish like him all the more—it was just the way Bar-Nun had described one of his most lovable and modest characters. That gesture alone made Shultish float on air.

Bar-Nun offered him cognac and cookies. Shultish's head swam, both from the liquor and from the writer's presence. Before Shultish had a chance to tell Bar-Nun about his translation of "The Yemenite Girl" the writer suddenly said, "Thank God, my stories are being translated. But each nationality has its own way of dealing with them. The Germans ask permission before they translate, and then send a copy; the Polacks ask for permission and never send; and the Americans neither ask for permission nor send."

Although he was not American, German, or Polish, but like Bar-Nun a Russian Jew from Odessa, Shultish had not asked permission to translate the story, and did not remove it from his jacket pocket. He always regretted this, for he was certain that it was a good translation, and with Bar-Nun's approval he could have become his classic translator into German.

"Are you planning a new collection this year?" Shultish asked.

Bar-Nun did not answer the question, for the phone rang, and when he put the receiver down, someone was at the door. "Bialik just called. God bless them, they don't leave me alone for a minute," Bar-Nun complained. "I have to run away from the house. The phone doesn't stop ringing. That's my punishment for not being in the Land of Israel. People keep coming all day long. Yesterday Gershoni, today Fichman. I tell you, it's the *Westbahnhof!*"

"You're the center of attention, *Adon* Bar-Nun. You're a famous man." Shultish wanted to add that he was sure he would win the Nobel Prize someday, but felt it was too presumptuous for an eighteen-year-old youth. Ah, if he had only said it then, how different his relationship with Bar-Nun would have been.

"Yes. But one can't write in a railroad terminal."

Like everyone who met him once, Shultish became a zealous guardian of Bar-Nun's privacy, considering it a waste of the old man's valuable time if anyone other than he went to visit the writer. In later years, when students or younger colleagues thought out loud in his presence of going to "drop in" on the old man when in Haifa, Shultish discouraged them, playing upon their conscience by reminding them that every hour Bar-Nun spent with them was an hour lost for Hebrew literature.

And now the rondo, A, B, A, was coming to full circle. When he first met Bar-Nun he had wanted to give him "The Yemenite Girl." And now, thirty-two years later, Bar-Nun was giving that same story to him. And what's more, his prediction had come true. Proud, and with a sense of personal triumph, Shultish felt that Bar-Nun's prize was as much his own doing as the writer's. After all, his book on Bar-Nun—the one he had not even wanted to write—had been published six months before the Nobel Prize. The people in Sweden must somehow—perhaps through the Chief Rabbi of Sweden—have taken notice, for the official announcement had mentioned language and style. But a rabbi's remark at Shultish's Bar-Nun lecture pleased him even more.

Shultish stood on the podium, analyzing "The Yemenite Girl." The stage was lit, the audience in semidarkness. Through Bar-Nun, Shultish was the center of attention. He and Bar-Nun and the Yemenite girl. Eyes on the audience, not down at his notes, Shultish recited—chanted, almost—the opening lines, then spoke about the story. As with most of Bar-Nun's works, ladies and gentlemen, this story, the love of a simple Yemenite girl for a European Jew, is symbolically complex and can be interpreted on many levels. Note the allusions in the opening lines. The image of the swarthy girl from the Song of Songs—"Look not upon me that I am swarthy, that the sun has tanned me"—sets the mood of love and hint of mysticism. The wine—"thy love is better than wine"—and the light going toward Jerusalem at sunset prepare the reader for the interplay of religious motifs. On another level, the story tells of the fusion of two old constrasting Jewries, dark and white; and on still another, it hints at how sophisticated Ashkenazi-European culture in Israel overwhelms the more primitive and passionate Jews from the Middle East. Finally, on the mystical level, like the Song of Songs itself, the story can be interpreted as the love between Israel and God.

The rabbi declared that Professor Shultish was probably the one American responsible for Bar-Nun's prize. For the first time in his life Shultish felt the thrill of being recognized. Yes indeed, he had been thinking this all along. He felt embarrassed at hearing it, considering it typical rabbinic exaggeration. But it was true after all. In a sense, then, he had forged Bar-Nun's destiny and, so to speak, owned a part of him.

Nevertheless, Bar-Nun was shared by others. Once Shultish came at the appointed time and found Emanuel Gutman there, an acquaintance of his from Haifa who had edited an anthology of Jerusalem folklore. Bar-Nun's welcome was more effusive than usual. He grasped both of Shultish's hands, and Shultish thought for a moment that the old man would kiss him. "Ah, *yedidi,* so glad to see you. Don't rush off, Gutman, I'm going up to the library for a minute. Remember I once promised to show you something? Shultish, please make yourself at home. The cognac is on the table, the cookies are in the bowl."

When Bar-Nun had gone up the stairs, Shultish asked, "Have you ever been up there, Gutman?"

"Where? The library? No."

"Me neither. People say it's the most fantastic view in Israel. . . . What's the matter? Why so restless?"

"My sister's coming from Canada and I'm supposed to meet her at the port. But now I have to wait for the old man to show me something."

Bar-Nun walked slowly down the stairs, holding an old quarto with a frayed two-tone leather binding. "Gutman, see this book? Now listen carefully, for I am doing you a favor, securing your rightful place in heaven. There can be no greater mitzvah, right, Shultish?"

"Absolutely."

"You know, Gutman, that my source book on Palestinian folklore is very widely read, not owing to any of my abilities, God forbid, but thanks to the sacred attributes of the Holy Land and the Jews' eternal interest in it. When in your book you quote the lengthy story of the eighteenth-century Jerusalem sage whom the sultan permitted to see the Cave of Machpelah in Hebron, you use as your source—"

Bar-Nun stopped and looked for a moment at Gutman, then gazed at Shultish too. Not that his eyes were focused on Shultish; on the contrary, they were fixed on the old tome he held in his hands. Nevertheless, Shultish felt Bar-Nun staring at him. Gutman's face, meanwhile, had turned deep red, then, suddenly, white.

"—this edition of Reb Yosele Galanter's memoirs, published in 1732. See? Take a good look at it. Note the fine, if somewhat frayed, leather binding. Also, please, the title page. I wanted to show it to you so that when you go up to heaven and the investigating angels ask you if you've seen Reb Yosele's memoirs, at least you'll be telling the truth if you say yes. But no matter, many writers have lifted sections from my *Folklore of Palestine*, along with the sources, without realizing that in many cases I've condensed, edited, translated Aramaic into Hebrew, or made lumpy Hebrew smooth. So it always amuses me to see these coincidences of careful editing being duplicated in other people's works. But never mind, Gutman *yedidi*, I bear no grudge. On the whole your work is a fine one—I've seen excellent reviews—and you deserve the Fichman Prize you're getting for it."

"Mazel tov!" Shultish jumped up, extending his hand to Gutman. "What wonderful news! I had heard a rumor that Firkovich was up for it."

"Firkovich!" Bar-Nun sniffed. "He specializes in putting out books that no one wrote and no one reads."

Shultish was intrigued by the paradoxical phrase, but he didn't want to ask Bar-Nun about it lest he encroach upon private knowledge or gossip, which he had no interest in. In any case, Bar-Nun would evade the question, and Shultish would be left wriggling on the hook of his own question mark.

After Gutman's departure Bar-Nun spoke about Reb Yosele's saintliness and honesty, retelling stories and legends that he had included in his own work and embellishing them. Shultish wondered how such an old man could remember, articulate, invent with such ease. Shultish wanted to talk about Stockholm and the prize, but Bar-Nun talked about Jerusalem and Safed. Shultish wanted to ask about his love stories; Bar-Nun spoke about the folklore of Palestine. It was for his writings on the Land of Israel, drawn from countless religious texts, that Bar-Nun wanted to be remembered; like Boccaccio, Petrarch, and Chaucer, he did not want to be remembered for his love stories.

Shultish left Bar-Nun's house happy that there had been no other visitors after Gutman. He went through the arbor and stepped out the gate. His heart at ease, Shultish was walking down the quiet street lined with thick eucalyptus trees when from behind

TEMPLE ISRAEL LIBRARY

one of them a man suddenly sprang out and collided with him, frightening Shultish out of his wits.

"Shultish, don't worry, it's me. I wanted to talk to you."

"Gutman, what are you doing here? You left"—he looked at his watch—"twenty minutes ago. To get your sister."

"The boat's not coming in till much later. I had to talk to you. To someone. I'm seething. Don't know what to do with myself. I was just walking around here, getting rid of nervous energy. I knew you'd be leaving soon. He doesn't have visitors after six-thirty. Imagine his gall. A *very* pious man. He had to do it in front of you. Couldn't do it in the half hour that we—"

"Half hour? You spent a half hour with him? Alone?"

"—we were together. Yes, of course we spent a half hour alone. What else? It was a blunder on my part. Completely unintentional. I had copied out his story to compare it with the original, then in the vast paper work—do you know what a job it was to sort out thousands of folk stories and legends?—it got thrown in and I didn't realize that I hadn't yet gone back to the original. I dare him to find another one I copied. If he had found another he would have mentioned it. He probably spent days poring over that book to find— Shaming a man in front of his friend. A specialty of his. But he doesn't forget to pray three times a day, and he always makes sure that like the pope he's photographed with his yarmulke on. *Very* pious. He's talking about my going up to heaven. After what he did to me just now he won't get twelve inches off the ground. He who shames his fellow man in public, says the Talmud, loses his share of the world to come. You know what it takes for a man to purposely wait for a man's friend to show up and then give him the wrong impression of me? The truth is, he was lying."

"Never mind, Gutman. He didn't really mean anything by it. After all, he congratulated you for the Fichman Prize. Said you deserved it."

"So what? He pats with one hand and slaps with the other. He has a special talent for nastiness."

"What did he mean that Firkovich specializes in putting out books no one wrote and no one reads?"

"Don't you know?"

"No. How should I know? If I knew I wouldn't ask."

"And Bar-Nun accuses me! There is a certain Reader of Judaica at a certain religion department in a certain island Kingdom who has had every one of his books and articles researched and written for him right here in Israel. The only thing he does write—is his name on the title page. It's disgusting."

"And Firkovich isn't even Jewish!" Shultish said.

"Firkovich happens to be a Karaite Jew of Egyptian descent. Go tell the Karaites they aren't Jews. Go start another schism."

"You *are* talking about Firkovich, Gutman. He holds the Sir Alfred Moscowitz Memorial Chair at Liv—"

"I'm not mentioning names. Committees consisting of poor rabbis and yeshiva students can't write books. Now you understand Bar-Nun's statement. But he isn't the only one . . ."

"I know," Shultish said. "I myself have heard there's a—"

"You'll excuse me, Shultish, but I've listened to enough gossip. Now I really do have to catch a bus down to the port. My sister is coming for the prize ceremonies. You'll come, won't you?"

"What a question. Where is it?"

"You mean I didn't send you an invitation?"

"No."

"Oy, I'm so sorry. I'll have one in the mail tomorrow. It'll be in Tel Aviv. Here's my bus."

"I'll tell you what," Shultish said, boarding the bus after him, "I'm in no rush to get home. I'll ride down with you. I love to watch the bay coming into view and disappearing as the bus serpentines down the side of the mountain."

"Shultish, you're a poet! And I thought you were only a scholar."

"Thank you. I write short stories, too. The view is especially beautiful at evening, when the lights gradually go on. Then city lights and starlight blend in the distance. But it takes a visitor to really appreciate it."

"True. I hardly notice it anymore."

"Tell me, Gutman, are you inviting Bar-Nun to the award ceremony?"

Gutman almost leaped out of his seat in sheer surprise. "Are you mad? Or do you think I'm crazy? Look, the Fichman is an important prize, one of the most important in Israel, and even second-rate writers pray to a God they have long rejected that Bar-Nun won't accept their invitation to attend the award ceremonies. His presence at a ceremony is like a kiss of death to the awardee. Bar-Nun knows this and uses his love sparingly, doling it out to those mediocre writers he despises the most. Sometimes, as a special bonus, he even attends the ceremonies of the big writers who win the big prizes, like the Fichman, if he's invited. His greatest coup was to attend the lavish ceremony for Malkiel Gritzer—"

"Oh, yes! The Hozenhausen Prize!"

"Right. A big fat three-thousand-dollar prize which only an American college with its rich donors can afford. You see, Bar-Nun attends public affairs so rarely that when he does show up in public, everyone's eyes are on him, and he knows it. After all, he's Bar-Nun, the living legend, and what's more, a Nobel Laureate. Anyway, when Gritzer got the Hozenhausen Prize, Bar-Nun gladly attended, not because Gritzer invited him; he didn't; they haven't gotten along in years. In fact, years ago, when Gritzer and Bar-Nun were invited by Ben-Gurion to go by helicopter from Haifa to Rehovot for a birthday celebration in honor of President Weitzmann, Bar-Nun in his inimitable style baited Gritzer so skillfully that Gritzer had a heart attack right on the helicopter. So you can see why Gritzer wouldn't invite Bar-Nun. But since Bar-Nun won the Hozenhausen Prize four years ago, the award committee invited him as a previous winner. Just by sitting there with that innocent look in his green eyes he bedazzled the audience and judges alike. First there were a few speeches of welcome, and then the head judge got up to present the award. He told about the history of the prize and praised its donors, Mr. and Mrs. Fishel Hozenhausen, who were onstage, the Mrs. with a corsage pinned to her bosom as if *she* were getting the prize. And then the judge got down to the presentation. 'And so,' he said, 'we present the Hozenhausen Distinguished Hebrew Novel Award to you—' Just then Bar-Nun sneezed, or coughed, or pretended to. The flustered judge, distracted by the noise, looked for a second at Bar-Nun in the first row, and said, 'to you, Yehiel Bar-Nun, for writing the finest Hebrew novel of the year.' And now you know why I'm rushing to invite him to the Fichman Prize ceremonies. I wouldn't even want him in the last row, that wicked old man!"

"Not so," said a voice from the seat behind them. Shultish felt a tap on the shoulder. Gutman turned too. A bearded man with earlocks leaned forward. "Excuse me," he whispered, tilting back his black fedora. "Fishbein is my name. I heard what the gentleman said, and it is not so."

"You know him, or you've just read his works?" Shultish asked.

"I know him. I know him. And you're wrong, sir, in what you said. Bar-Nun is a *lamed vovnik,* one of the thirty-six hidden saints on whose existence the world depends."

"Bar-Nun a *lamed vovnik!*" Gutman burst out laughing. "Bar-Nun is a *lamed vovnik* like I'm a fig tree."

"I don't want to tell this story," Fishbein said, "but I have to. Bar-Nun surely doesn't want this story publicized, but I'm sorry, I can't sit silently and let this saintly man be slandered. What he did for my fam—"

"Do saints shame their—?" Gutman began, but Shultish pinched his leg.

"Oh, Herzl Street, my stop." Gutman rose and ran out the door. "You'll tell me about it, Shultish," he shouted as the door closed.

"All right, I promise. . . . Why did he run out here? This isn't the port."

The bus stopped for a red light. Shultish looked out the window. In the bus Gutman had run; as soon as he touched the sidewalk his haste was switched off, as if he had pulled an emergency brake on himself. A moment later he stood beside a young woman and tapped her shoulder. The girl turned in surprise, and with an automatic gesture patted Gutman's arm for a moment. The bus moved; Shultish craned his neck, gazing at the beautiful girl. A Yemenite beauty. What was Gutman doing with a twenty-year-old girl? Shultish closed his eyes and saw her on the inside of his lids. Something stirred in him, invisible gears attempting to lock into

37

place. Gears of sunbeams and gold. But there was a mixup here. An error of destiny. It was he who should have met this lovely girl, not homely Gutman. What was Gutman, a married man, doing with her? And Shultish could not even question Gutman about the girl, for he could not embarrass Gutman. No matter how mild the tone, the question "Who was that pretty Yemenite?" would have a scornful, accusative ring. No wonder Gutman was in such a rush to get off the bus. To get to folklore. Tap the source. When he turned back to the man with the beard, ready now to hear his story, the man was gone. Another burden to carry, Shultish thought. An insult to a pious Jew.

I don't know what the Yemenite girl did. I don't know whether she worked and came only after work; or whether she was not employed at all. Perhaps she was a rich merchant's daughter and had the time to loll by the sea, or perhaps she was a poor cobbler's child who could find no employment and, to compensate for her sorrow, came to bathe in a water that soothes all sorrow. I don't know what the Yemenite girl did; what I did, I know.

After work I would come to the sea to let my body and my spirit relax. I walked on my heels on the damp sand licked by the tide and watched the little white halos that disappeared as soon as they were formed. Even on a day when I ceased work early and came at eleven, she would be there too. Perhaps it was coincidence that we shared our hours, but then again perhaps her hours of work were as odd as mine.

Shultish switched on the light. He picked up the Israeli edition of his book, admired its jacket and title page, and continued looking for typos that could be corrected in a future printing. But he could read no more than a page, for his thoughts were wandering and there was a fuzzy feeling inside his head, as though an endless stream of soda bubbles were floating by. He turned the light off. Maybe all this had begun that evening he spent with Bar-Nun, Gutman, and Fishbein with the beard: the bus rides, fatigue, night air, lowered resistance, and talking for hours about Bar-Nun.

What made the old man so popular? Why couldn't any literary conversation be conducted without the mention of his name? Bar-Nun never went to symposia, never lectured, never taught; unlike all other writers of Hebrew fiction, Bar-Nun did not write criticism for the Friday literary supplements, or journalism or humorous poetry to keep his name and wit before the public; he was not a panelist on radio shows, or an interviewee on interview shows. Nevertheless, by his silence he had become a public personality; a rare appearance at a book award ceremony, a visit to the President's house for a literary evening—where it was said he sat in the front row with a slightly pained expression, glancing at his watch occasionally when the speeches got too long—and his picture was in all the papers.

After presenting Bar-Nun with the Israeli edition of his book, Shultish had felt particularly euphoric and asked the old man about his views on literature. Bar-Nun usually evaded these questions with ambiguities or generalities. This time, however, Bar-Nun spoke at length. Shultish could not understand why Bar-Nun had suddenly graced him with this favored treatment. The only answer could be that he was very pleased by Shultish's book—the first devoted to Bar-Nun's style and diction.

"We talk about literature," Bar-Nun said. "We puff it up; we blow hard on the balloon until we begin to believe our own exaggerations that this is a great literature. Do you know what it is? It is rotting bones, and no new Ezekiel is in sight to resurrect it. There are one, maybe two good writers of Hebrew today. We don't realize how poor our literature is until we see it in translation and compare it to other work being done in that language. Oh yes, it is published abroad. As a courtesy, as pro-Israel sentiment, but never as art. A literature lives only when it stands up in translation . . ."

The phone rang.

"Ah, I said the nasty word: translation. Now I'm punished with a call. . . . Yes. . . . Who?" Bar-Nun smiled. He spoke in monosyllables. It was difficult to construct the conversation from the old man's few words.

A literature lives only when it stands up in translation. This view surprised Shultish. He had once read that Bar-Nun had said just the opposite, that only those works that have been translated into Hebrew were secure for eternity. Bar-Nun's famous utterance had been: "Dante will survive. He is safe. We have him in Hebrew now."

Bar-Nun hung up. "Yarkoni. You know him?"

Shultish could not tell by Bar-Nun's face whether he should say yes enthusiastically or admit only to an acquaintance. "I've heard of him. He's a translator."

"They're all alike, these nudniks, eager to take a man's works and translate them. Once a man gets hold of a pen, he thinks he can tell it what to do. But the pen usually masters its master. Only in rare exceptions is the pen subdued. These translators! First they say 'I can write my name.' Thus they establish that they are literate. Then they conveniently drop the last two words and proclaim themselves as writers to the world."

He's talking about me, Shultish thought.

"Does Yarkoni want to translate your stories?" he asked quickly.

"Who doesn't? He thinks one success in translation automatically breeds another."

"What did he translate?"

" 'The Yemenite Girl.' Into German. Published in a Swiss anthology recently."

Shultish's head spun. His heart spiraled. He saw Bar-Nun through a blur.

"My God. I had a translation of that story in my pocket when I first met you in Vienna thirty-two years ago."

"Why didn't you show it to me? I would have made you my German translator."

"I was too shy. And now my German is useless. . . . Did I hear you say a literature lives only when it stands up in translation?"

"Yes. That's why I like good translations. A good work can be translated. We have to touch others with our work. Don't believe those who say, 'Bar-Nun has a certain magic that you just cannot translate.' Nonsense! Every writer can be translated. He just has to find his genius of a translator."

Shultish blushed, assuming he'd been insulted again; his eyes brimmed involuntarily. He felt guilty for not having been successful in translating Bar-Nun.

"But how about the Hebrew masters of the nineteenth and early twentieth centuries?" Shultish asked. "And the nineteenth-century periodicals that gave them their first organ of expression and encouraged them?"

Bar-Nun grimaced, waved his hand. "Masters? Junk! What language, what style! The dull ennui of Gershoni. The claptrap of Klaperstein. It could have been published only in Hebrew. The literature was then a hundred and fifty years behind the culture of the West. It was—and is now—narcissistic and narrow when it worked from its own traditions and themes, and ludicrous and imitative when it sought to flee them. Don't you agree, Shultish?"

Questioned again. He blinked away Gershoni's Christmas tree, had it on the tip of his tongue to offer it as a tidbit of gossip to Bar-Nun, but restrained himself. Shultish didn't know what to say. To betray his life work, the inherent dignity of his own discipline, his entire being here on earth?

"It's true," Shultish said. "I've been thinking it all along but never dared utter it."

He looked at Bar-Nun. The old man's tiger-green eyes urged him to continue.

"What do you think of the younger writers?" Shultish asked.

"I don't have the time to read them. People are always sending me books that just pile up. Who has the time for all this? I wish— no, no, don't look so depressed, Shultish, I don't mean your book. Books by people like you are always welcome. They tell me what I did. Sometimes even what I wanted to do but didn't know I was doing. That's even cleverer. But your book is an important work, I should say a *very* important work. And I know you write fiction too."

"Thank you. Thank you very much. You don't know what a statement like that means to me. But since you mentioned that you

41

liked the book, I was wondering if you have heard . . . I mean, perhaps since you're in touch with so many people . . . if my book, now that it has appeared in Israel, has been nominated for any of the prizes. . . ." Even a little one, from some little town like Holon, would do, he thought. Yes, even the Holon Prize would satisfy him.

Bar-Nun smiled. "I know nothing. What do I know about these things? But do you want to hear my opinion? If I were you, I wouldn't be so eager for one of these literary prizes. Literary prizes bring all sorts of headaches. For example, because I won a certain big prize, everyone wants to see me. Now they are going to drag a sick old man all over Europe so that I can be put on exhibition."

"Really? What interesting news. When are you leaving?"

"I'll see. I don't know yet. Maybe in two weeks if I feel well. You see? Prizes. Headaches. Brought on only by pride. Our writers are very proud. Our literary supplements are constantly full of praises for our own writers. And thank God there's no shortage of literary awards. There's always something for someone. Every day there's another prize being awarded, or a committee-in-the-making to dream up a new one. Shultish, believe me, it's a mark of distinction for a writer *not* to get one. Israel is a tiny land, the writer-judges know one another, and social and political considerations rule over literary ones. You want to hear a story?"

"You know your stories always fascinate me," Shultish said with forced calm, immediately overcome by terror lest his words trigger another remark like "I'll tell you some other time; I'm tired now."

But to Shultish's great delight Bar-Nun continued: "If you lived here you'd soon realize all this yourself."

"You see," Shultish explained, "I feel I'm doing my duty to the Jewish people by teaching Hebrew literature in the Diaspora. That's why I don't live in Israel. We must keep Hebrew alive abroad, too. Where do you find good teachers nowadays?"

Bar-Nun clapped his hands in contrition. "Oy, God forbid that you should wrongly interpret my remarks. I'm not like those others who make Diaspora Jews feel guilty by saying, 'Why don't you live in Israel? Your place is here.' Every Jew has a right to live where he likes, even if it isn't Israel. Especially a man who devotes his life to the literature, as you, my dear friend, are doing. I meant merely that you are far away and don't know all the little machinations involved in literary prizes. Would you like to know how they work?''

"All right," Shultish said hesitantly, careful not to sound too eager.

"Now listen carefully. It goes something like this. Frumkin is seventy-seven and hasn't yet gotten a national literary prize, only a few of the local city prizes, garbage ones like Dimona, Ashdod, and other godforsaken towns. The committee—an inner club: the faces change, the expression remains the same—consisting of writers like Lumkin, Zumkin, and Patemkin, meets somewhere in Tel Aviv. One of the judges, Zumkin, sits back, takes a puff on his imported cigarette—writers are fond of imported cigarettes—and says: 'Let's give Frumkin the Ussishkin Prize this year.' 'No,' says Patemkin, 'Cohen has been after the Ussishkin for years. He needs it to round out the Big Four, since he already has the Brenner, Bialik, and Tchernihovsky.' But the third judge, Lumkin—''

Wasn't all this out of one of his satires? Shultish thought. Was Bar-Nun reciting, reading, or living now? Shultish lifted his finger to turn an imaginary page. The shadow of his hand swerved across Bar-Nun's face.

"—Lumkin, you see, demurs. 'Why should Cohen get the Grand Slam? *I* don't have it yet. I don't even have the Bialik yet, and God knows I deserve it.' 'All right,' say the others, 'you approve Cohen for the Ussishkin and we'll get you the Bialik this year for criticism.' 'No,' says Lumkin. 'I don't want it for my criticism; I want it for my poetry.' To this they agree. For they are reasonable men. 'All right, then, it's settled. Cohen gets the Ussishkin, and you, Lumkin, will get the Bialik.' 'For my poetry.' 'For your poetry. That leaves us with only Frumkin. He's seventy-seven and deserves a prize. But, between us, Frumkin is a third-rate writer, so let's get him a third-rate award like the Fichman Prize.' In other words, the sort of prize the Gutmans deserve. I hope you don't think that the story of Reb Yosele was the only legend he lifted. There were others, but I didn't want to embarrass him. Isn't Fichman terrible?"

"The prize or the poet-critic?" Shultish asked.

"The writer, of course. I *know* what your opinion of third-rate prizes is. I refer to Fichman the scribbler."

"Fichman!" Shultish snorted. "An impressionist. Creating flowers and rhetoric around other writers instead of solid literary criticism. He gives me knots in my stomach."

Bar-Nun nodded, pleased.

"So everyone agreed that Frumkin would get the Fichman, until Zumkin remembered that Frumkin was serving on the judging committee of the Fichman Prize this year. Giving oneself the literary prize of which one was not a judge was immodest but not impossible; but giving oneself the prize of which one *was* the judge was rather inconvenient. Poor public relations. See? We've learned something from you Americans. Public relations."

"Then which prize did poor Frumkin finally get?"

"Poor Frumkin finally got the one he deserved. The poor Holon Prize."

Shultish tried to sleep but knew the attempt would be futile. Soon his wife should return. She couldn't be away much longer. He shifted from side to side, his mind ablaze.

The phone rang. His wife calling. He answered the second ring.

"Shultish? Gutman."

"Ah, Gutman. I got sick. That's why I couldn't come to your affair. I'm sorry."

He craned his neck, saw Gutman's Yemenite girl friend walking up the street. The bus started. She moved out of his sight. Holding hands with Gutman? He closed his eyes, weary. The girl was there again, swimming into view.

"Hello? Shultish? Are you there?"

"Yes, yes."

"I heard you were ill, Shultish. How are you doing?"

"Coming along. Slowly. It's a long process. What can one do?"

"You know, I never heard the end of that Hasid's story about Bar-Nun. Remember? On the bus."

"Yes. You ran off. No end to the story." He opened his eyes. Was it the bus that moved, or the girl? Or perhaps both at the same time. "I don't have the strength to explain now. Let me call you in the morning. I expect my wife home any minute. You'll be home?"

"Till nine-thirty."

"How was the ceremony?"

"Fine. All the famous people were there."

"Bar-Nun too?"

Gutman laughed. "Well, not *all* the famous people, thank God. I don't need *all* the famous people. Just some of them."

So Gutman still hadn't forgotten his grudge against Bar-Nun. Shultish looked up at the ceiling, white and tranquil, the screen for all his thoughts. For decades he had thought that Bar-Nun was the greatest writer in the world. When he was thirteen Shultish had received as a Bar Mitzvah present a three-volume set of Bar-Nun's works—published in their native Odessa—and he had loved the man before he ever met him. He loved him through his books, saw the kind of man he was by the kind of men he wrote about— tender, genteel, men of superb moral refinement. But years later, when he began to read Bar-Nun in translation, he had noted the limitations of his narrative. Bar-Nun's stories were framed neatly into the Hebrew itself; removed from it they were rather bloodless, involuted and, yes, boring, especially the novels that had been mentioned by the Nobel Prize committee. As more of Bar-Nun's books appeared in English, American critics had begun to treat him in critical fashion. Gone was the adulation of the honeymoon period just after the Nobel Prize. At first, when critics thrashed the great novels as dull, Shultish had considered it a personal insult. If the writer was Jewish, he was a Jewish anti-Semite; if Christian, a plain goyisher anti-S*emitt.* Gradually, however, Shultish had seen that they were right. If the greatest figure in modern Hebrew literature was dull, what was the rest of the literature worth? Ages ago it had made a ripple on the world scene, bringing like a newborn soul both good and evil into the world. But now?

Shultish wanted to lift the phone. He knew he had the energy, but somehow he could not bring himself to move to the other side of the bed. The line would be busy anyway. Soon he would close his eyes and dream of his wife in double image and of the honey-colored long-haired girl swimming naked in the pool.

It was getting dark. Down in the bay of Haifa illuminated ships were bobbing on the water. In Israel there were no twilights. At sunset darkness arched over the world.

I am not the sort who pushes himself on others; born in Nicolsburg, I share my forefathers' values of propriety and grace. When asked if I am kin to the famous Hasid, Reb Shmelke of Nicolsburg, I lower my head and do not deny it. I say this not out of vanity, but out of loyalty to my saintly ancestor and to my town. For cities, like families, have a character, and they lend to its sons the things they learn. And so, because I stem from Nicolsburg, I did not rush to her; I did not preen like a peacock and come to conquer. I have seen friendships quickly formed and quickly broken. I know life on the beach; I know its rhythms; its rhythms are as alluring and powerful as the unending rush and ebb of water to shore. My rhythms are slower and, I hope, longer lasting.

The door slammed.

"Thank God you're home. Are you all right?" he said before he saw her. "I was afraid something had happened."

His wife sat down on the chair at the foot of his bed.

"Well, did you bring my Yemenite?"

Then he saw, even in the dark, that she had been crying. Her face had that puffy look that immediately drew sympathy and love.

"The Yemenite!" she said. "Can you imagine what I just went through? First you sick, then Clara in Lugano, and now this."

"Did something happen in town? I missed the news, but I didn't hear any ambulances."

"Nothing like that. Just the worst encounter I've ever had with another human being."

"You didn't get the tape," Shultish said.

"I knocked on the door. It opened, and before I had a chance to say hello a woman shrieked at me: 'What do you want? Who gave you permission to come here?' Bar-Nun's daughter-in-law is a red-haired freckle-faced woman. When a redhead is pretty she can be stunning, but when she's ugly and freckled and has frizzly hair, her face can stop a clock. I was sucked into the apartment by the force of her voice and swing of the door and the sheer surprise of her welcome. 'My husband spoke to your husband, and he said I could come,' I stuttered. She leaned back, opened up her yellow mouth, and laughed. 'Ha! My husband! That was my son. A thirteen-year-old boy! You take a thirteen-year-old boy's word? Is a thirteen-year-old boy responsible?' 'My husband said he spoke to Bar-Nun's son. I assumed he meant the writer's son.' For goodness' sake, Ezra, why didn't you tell me you spoke to a thirteen-year-old boy?"

"I told you I spoke to Bar-Nun's son. I told you I was calling the son in the first place. So that Bar-Nun's son means the grandson of the writer."

"Well, how should I know this? So she said, 'My husband is Bar-Nun too, unfortunately. The name brings joy to some, but misery to us. Look around the apartment. Do you see a maid's touch here? No, of course you don't, because everything is done by me, by my own hands, after I come home from work. We can't afford a maid. My husband drives down to Tel Aviv every day, and that boy is left alone here after school. Bar-Nun has an unlisted number. People come here from all over the world to meet the famous writer and call us because we're the only Bar-Nun in the Haifa directory. He lives there on the very top of the Carmel in peace and prosperity, and we get the phone calls. He forbids us to give anyone his number, and yet people call from American television, the BBC, and especially the Scandinavian networks. They think they have a monopoly on him because of the Nobel Prize. All of them are sent here to see him, but without consulting him first. They just feel they'll get to him. So my boy answers the phone. People tell him it's a matter of life and death. The boy gets frightened and gives them Bar-Nun's number.'

"By this time I was drawn into her messy living room, and we managed to find a place to sit. She brushed the wild red hair out of her eyes and continued: 'They get their interview, their story, their film, whatever they're after, and the old man grumbles to us but enjoys every minute of it, then nags us to death for giving them his phone number. He's promised hundreds of times to get his number listed, but he never does. Why doesn't he list his number and hire a secretary to take his calls? He can afford it. Especially after the prize. My God, sixty thousand dollars! Meantime we serve as his clearing house. He does that constantly. Don't you know him? Haven't you read his stories? Don't you realize what a complex man he is? Just read his works. He's exactly the same way in real life. He operates on a dozen levels simultaneously and is in full control of each one. Look, we have our own lives . . .' "

"Stop shouting," Shultish said. "I have a headache. . . ."

"I'm sorry, Ezra, but that's the way she spoke. 'My husband can't live in the perpetual shadow of his famous father. I won't let him. He could have been a writer; he had plenty of talent. But I didn't want him to compete with the old man. So he became an assistant to an architect. Drives in every day to and from Tel Aviv. He works hard; he's not well. I can hear you asking me why we don't move to Tel Aviv. Why drive down from the middle of the Carmel to Haifa, which alone takes half an hour, and then the seventy-five minutes to Tel Aviv if you do ninety kilometers an hour and if the traffic is good? Why? Again the old man. My husband feels it's his duty to be near him. How can he live in Tel Aviv if his old father is in Haifa? True, he has two other daughters, and his other son is the Ambassador to Switzerland. But no matter. A son is a son, right? And does a son leave an eighty-two-year-old father, even if he is the picture of health? You want an example of how the old man operates? One day we make arrangements for him to come to us for supper. I leave work early to prepare, because as you know he's very picky: fresh fruits, only the white meat of tender chickens, stewed vegetables without salt, Iraqi pitta and couscous which I have to run down to the city market for. Served at five. It takes special preparing and shopping. My hus-band loses half a day's work to drive in from Tel Aviv up to the summit of the Carmel to bring him down so that supper can begin at five. He comes to Bar-Nun, and the old man pulls a sour face and says: "You know what, Moshe? Not today. I just . . . some-how today I just don't feel like it. Why don't you pick me up tomorrow instead?" The only one he thinks of is himself. You'd think he would ask how I feel when he talks to my husband. Never.' "

"I don't believe her," Shultish said. "She must be lying. The very first words he inevitably utters are: 'How is your wife, your family?' He does that over the phone and in person."

"'You see what we have to contend with? And to top it off, tapes! There's a pile of tapes in that room, some ours, some his, and they're not even sorted. People borrow tapes and never return them. He won't record for anyone, and whenever anyone asks him he says, "See my son. My son has a copy of that story." It may be true and it may not be true. We've got lots of them, and they're not catalogued. And you can't always believe him. Whatever he says, look for the irony in it. If you've once heard him say, "Ah, yedidi, I'm so glad you called," you can be sure he's enraged at being disturbed. He's a tricky old man who plays with other people. When he says black he means white, and vice versa. Have you ever heard his views on Hebrew literature? Ha! Watch out that you carefully interpret his remarks. Or the way he corners people into saying things they never dreamed of saying.'

"Ezra, I tell you, I sat there stunned while she raved on. I couldn't say a word. When finally the anger rose in me and I opened my mouth, I felt myself gagging. 'Is this the way you receive visitors?' I said to her. The flight bag with the tape recorder in it dangled from my hand. I didn't know where to begin—to tell her about your being sick, leaving you alone, to let her know what you've done for Bar-Nun. And then I did a foolish thing. The tension in me just snapped and I began to cry. I just sat there bawling and trembling. That made her feel guilty and uncomfortable and she began to apologize."

"A brilliant stroke. Beautiful," Shultish said. "The one weapon women use is the one they are most vulnerable to. . . . One tear is worth a thousand words."

"'You have to realize how miserable our lives are because of him,' she said. 'He has the fame and we bear its burdens. He doesn't care about anyone. Why doesn't he publish his phone number and hire a secretary? My God, he made sixty thousand

49

dollars. That's a lifetime's income in one stroke. He could certainly afford it. But who knows what he did with his money? But oh no, he leaves his phone number as is. Lets us act as his secretary, then takes it out on us.' When I calmed down I told her, 'Do you think I just go popping into strangers' houses for no reason? That I don't have to tend to a sick husband who has been bedridden nearly two months, and a sick sister in Lugano I can't even go to now?' ''

"You'll go," Shultish said. "I promised myself. As soon as I'm better, you'll go!"

'' 'That he got sick in the first place because he was running around because of his interest in Bar-Nun, exhausting himself and coming down with a virus? That I'm making this story up?' She didn't say a word. Just looked at me sort of pathetically, then stared down at my open flight bag. 'Oh, you brought a tape recorder.' 'Well, what do you think?' I told her. 'You think I would come down here to take away your tape? My husband asked your son if I could come with a tape recorder to copy your tape and he said yes.' 'What does a thirteen-year-old boy know?' she said. 'He gets calls every day like this and always gives away the old man's number. Bar-Nun has a good time in the limelight, and then we eat our hearts out listening to his complaints.' I told her it was senseless to start this whole routine all over again. I went to the door, opened it, and made my first faux pas. On my part it was absolutely unintentional. After all, I had never seen the man.''

"What man?" Shultish asked.

"Bar-Nun. I've only seen pictures of him. You've never taken me to him."

"He's never told me to bring you."

"There's a way of getting an invitation."

"Please, Shoshana, not now. What happened?"

"As I stood by the doorway, I saw a man coming toward us and I told her, 'Look, here comes your father-in-law. Let's ask him. You'll see that he told my husband to ask you about the recording.' 'That's my *husband*,' she said. God, it was the same face, except where the old writer stood up straight and appeared self-confident, the son, about fifty I would say, was bent over, dejected, the world on his shoulders. I could see the father standing on his back, and the son was overpowered because he amounted to nothing, despite his continued proximity to Bar-Nun. That sickly shlimazel son of a successful father who married a Lady Macbeth in pants!''

"God, what a reception!" Shultish reached for the phone. "I'm going to call up that witch and give her a piece of my mind. Did you mention my name?"

"Yes."

"Did she recognize it?"

"No. What does she care about Hebrew literature? What do most people here care about it?"

"She doesn't know what I've done for him?"

"She couldn't care less. . . . Don't call, Ezra. She's a miserable woman whose life is embittered. It's eaten into her face and voice and being. Calling up won't do any good."

"And after all I've done for Bar-Nun, this is the way she treats me. Because, after all, you were representing me. What a way to treat a perfect stranger, to humiliate someone like that! Her father-in-law offers everyone cognac and cookies and she comes forth throwing salt in your eyes."

Shoshana was silent. He heard her breathing in the dark room. Outside the window, the crickets; one group vibrated steadily, another chirped in quick cycles. In the distance, the lights in the bay. I'm sorry, he wanted to tell his wife, that I caused you so much pain. But the silence held him back. His wife's even breathing and the sounds of the crickets lulled him; weariness overwhelmed him and he let himself sleep.

Deep in sleep he did not dream of his wife or of the girl in the pool. Deep in sleep, floating in a stream where opposing currents met, he wondered what to do with his life. Questioned, the will replied. He slept, peacefully at first, then tossed about, dreaming of living waters rising.

I knew the Yemenite girl long before I knew her. I do not play with words, or with paradoxes. There are three levels of knowing:

the outer—of dress and mannerisms, the way the hair is combed, a person's walk and gestures, the shape of his face when he is tranquil or angry; but all this is one-dimensional, seen from the outside, observed from afar, while the observer may still be a stranger. The second level of knowing is the one in which the observer also becomes observed, in which every word and gesture becomes question and answer, a game of two-part harmony. Here the dimensions increase from one to two or even three, depending on the depths of the people. The third kind of knowing is the most mysterious and intimate of all, when man knows woman, Adam Eve, in a net of ecstasy.

Reticent and shy by nature, I took my time in getting to know the Yemenite girl. First, because I thought I was destined to know her. Second, because she was always there, or almost always there. Only once did I feel her absence, when I sought the sea breeze one afternoon. I climbed the dune by the path-no-path I always used, looked down and saw empty space and sand in the place where she always sat. Seeing sand and emptiness, I thought of the desert.

TWO

Shultish, recuperating, felt like a Bar-Nun hero: alone in Israel, his family abroad. Shultish, recuperating. Shultish, searching. His wife was gone. Bar-Nun too. Yet even in absence there was contact. Shultish was an ingenious man. He needed only one hand for a handshake.

On the bus one evening—how odd: he had just been thinking of the man: Shultish had offended him by breaking off the conversation: he carried the pain of the insult: a knob of discomfort that occasionally surfaced—Shultish met the Hasid who had called Bar-Nun a saintly man.

"I have to apologize. I was distracted because my friend ran out. You were telling me—and then I looked—you weren't there. It bothered me. I insulted you. Forgive me."

The man made a deprecatory gesture with his hands. He stroked his beard, smoothed back his earlocks. Shultish could tell by his eyes, alive with fire and mirth, that the Hasid bore him no grudge.

"Do you want to hear the story now?" he asked Shultish.

"Of course I do. Come, sit next to me."

The man slid into the seat. "Have you seen Bar-Nun lately?"

"No. I've been ill. Bedridden for some weeks. But thank God I'm better."

"Now you'll have to wait until he comes back from Europe."

"Well, I did get regards from him. By coincidence, he and my wife took the same flight to Switzerland. So they finally got to meet. When he found out that my wife was visiting her sick sister, he immediately offered the assistance of his son the Ambassador."

"You see? It seems that you know him the way I do. But it's for him, your friend, the one who ran off the bus that day, that I wanted to tell the story. But since you promised to tell him, I'll tell you. You must have read about me in the papers, the Fishbein family. We have eight children—may they live and be well—and I work for a bookstore that sells religious goods. The point is, though, that my wife has a kidney ailment and needed a kidney machine."

"Yes." Shultish remembered vaguely. "In the papers, about three months ago."

"Exactly. Those machines cost ten thousand pounds. And where can a man like me, who barely earns four hundred pounds a month, which goes to feed the family, get ten thousand pounds? But without the machine my wife would have to be hospitalized. With it she can function normally in the house. It's a portable machine, you see. A modern miracle. A gift from the Almighty. Anyway, a reporter heard from a doctor at the Haifa hospital and came to write about us in the papers. . . . Here's my stop."

"I'll get off with you. Let's walk."

Shultish was perspiring with excitement. A sea breeze brought the scent of salt. A chill passed over him. Up on the Carmel he sensed the sea's magic, saw it from far away, a sheet of shimmering glass. Now he heard the incessant muted roar and smelled its salt; he tasted its dampness in the air.

"Didn't the papers report that a fund was started?"

"Yes, later, but there was no need for it. Did you hear anything about who paid for it? Aha! See? Of course not. After the article

56

was published some money started coming in. Tens and fifties, about seven hundred pounds in all, from good Jews who felt sympathy for another human being."

"How does Bar-Nun fit in?"

"Wait, you'll see. That's the point. The purpose! With Hasidim, you know, stories have a purpose. One night I heard a knock on the door, and guess who it was? Bar-Nun himself. He apologized for coming in unannounced but felt there was no other way. To make a long story short, he offered to buy the machine for my wife, but on the condition that it be done in strict anonymity. Naturally I refused. Not the anonymity. The gift. One man. Not a rich man. A writer who works for the entire house of Israel. 'Look,' he told me. 'Do you know how much money the Nobel Prize gave me?' I told him I didn't know. 'Guess,' he said. I guessed a thousand pounds. He laughed. 'It's not the Holon Prize for the Year's Best Book. It's sixty thousand.' 'Sixty thousand pounds?' I said. 'Dollars,' he said. 'That means two hundred ten thousand pounds. It is for this that God caused me to get the Nobel Prize. If the Holy Temple were standing on the Temple Mount in Jerusalem, I would run to it with ten percent of my prize as a tithe for the priests and Levites. Since the Holy Temple is not standing, I shall not take twenty-one thousand pounds but will give you ten thousand for the health of your wife. Would that the Holy Temple were standing, for if it were we would be in the Messiah's times, and your wife would be cured, for it is written that in the End of Days the ailing will become well. But since owing to our sins the Holy Temple has not been rebuilt and the Messiah has not yet come, you have ten thousand and I have saved eleven. So we both have realized a profit, mine perhaps greater than yours, for by your kindness in accepting you have permitted me to gain a mitzvah. May the Lord send health to your wife and to all the ailing in Israel.' He shook my hand, kissed the mezuza, and left. Now tell this story, as I told it to you, to that man who slandered a *lamed vovnik*, one of the thirty-six hidden saints of Israel."

Shultish crossed the street and waited for the bus to take him back up to the Carmel, where the lights of houses were brighter than stars. The wind was brisk, and he wore only a short-sleeved shirt. He had always thought that only the upper level of Haifa was cool. But the city was chilly too, especially at night. He shivered. Bar-Nun was right. A man should wear a topcoat in Haifa's evening air.

Shultish regained his strength by walking: a mile each day, with a map of Haifa in hand. He started slowly, and gradually increased the briskness, trying all sorts of walks—from the hips, from the legs, sometimes swinging his arms, sometimes not. When he was younger he had amused himself by imitating how friends walked, noting carriage, thrust of legs, position of head and shoulders; he could recognize a person at a distance by his walk. But what use was all that knowledge? It was like all the other bits of cleverness and useless information that mothers and fathers took pride in. Unlike gold, it could not be melted down into some general treasury of wisdom or creativity to be called upon in an hour of stress.

Shultish himself had a rather slow walk. Once, up Herzl Street, he saw a man walking toward him with a slightly rolling gait, a walk faintly familiar. He tried imitating it. Looking up, he found himself walking toward himself—his own reflection in a mirror at the corner of a shop.

Now that Bar-Nun had gone abroad, he would imitate *his* walk and become him. Slow down the pace. Shoulders slightly rounded, one shoulder forward, feet slightly out, like Charlie Chaplin. If only he were wearing a battered old wide-brimmed fedora, he would surely be mistaken for Bar-Nun. He imagined someone calling *Adon* Bar-Nun, *Adon* Bar-Nun, what are you doing here? I thought you were— and a finger tapping on his shoulder.

The doctor was right. Walking after so many weeks in bed was fine exercise. Shultish felt a new spirit in his limbs, the gradual surge of health. Where to now? He consulted his map to see if the radius of a mile cut across any friendships. A walk with a purpose. Although a walk with no purpose in Haifa was equally good. For wherever one turned, there were trees and parks and, in his neighborhood, the panorama of the U-shaped bay, from Acco to south of Haifa; steamships in the distance with their faint horns and columns of smoke, and the houses stepping down the mountainside, looking like a huge white stairway. In the evening the city had its own beauty. In the evening the lights of the city matched the starlight.

The closest person to his radius was Gutman. A leisurely fifteen-minute walk. Shultish had not visited him before, but there had to be a first time. What held him back was the girl. Suppose she was there when he dropped in one morning, while Gutman's wife was away teaching. What would Shultish say if he found her there? But if Gutman was smart he would hide her. Yes, that's what he would do if someone rang the bell. So there was no danger of her being in the living room when he came. Shultish walked confidently up to Gutman's house and rang the bell. The footsteps behind the door were too light to be Gutman's. He could recognize a person's walk even if he couldn't see him. Sound sufficed. And it wasn't Gutman's wife, either. Shultish's heart began knocking against his chest. A sour odor of fright wafted out of his shirt. Should he run, hide, dash up the stairs, even though he wasn't supposed to run? And if caught by the girl, gaze for a moment to fuse the real image with the one behind his lids, then beg pardon, wrong door?

Too late; door arcing open.

"Good morning," she said.

He looked at her honey skin, brown eyes, and perfectly shaped lips. A Yemenite Queen Esther, he thought. No more, no less. He looked down at the still-damp floor with its little islands of wetness where the tiles had settled somewhat. Others are doomed by water—and I, water has saved me again.

"Is *Adon* Gutman in?" he asked, buoyant.

"*Adon* Gutman is in his study. Do you want to come in? Excuse me, but the floor is still wet. I'm in the mid—"

"It's all right." Shultish beamed. "Perfectly all right. Tell him Shultish was here. I'll drop in again. . . . And you, what is your name?"

"Miriam."

A few days later, walking up the street to Gutman's house, Shultish smiled, laughed to himself. And I actually made homely Gutman a lover. Homely Gutman—and Miriam, the Yemenite maid. What a joke. Now that he had saved Gutman from adultery, Shultish enjoyed visiting him. Gutman at home was different from the way he'd been at Bar-Nun's. Less on edge, more confident, master of his house. And looking at Gutman's maid was not a bad diversion either. No artist should shun beauty; aesthetic needs demanded it. Seeing Gutman reminded Shultish of their visit to Bar-Nun. There was no way of reaching the old man now. Where was he today? Paris? London? Invited back to the scenes of his former triumphs. What new works would emerge from these visits? And who would translate them? Again Shultish saw himself walking toward himself. This time he recognized his image. He had not changed that much. Just a trifle thinner, perhaps. He patted his chest; his jacket hung a bit looser around the shoulders. When Shoshana returned she would remark on how well he looked.

Shultish stopped at the corner, waited for the little green man in the traffic light to appear, then dashed across the street. In Haifa cars didn't stop for people; people had to stop for them. As he walked the streets his eyes put a frame around each scene he saw and preserved it. A man carrying a block of ice, a sack draped over his shoulder—something out of the early forties in the Bronx. A little girl, with melting ice-cream cone in hand, showing her mother a tooth that had just come out. A boy in mid-flight, jumping off the low stone wall of a park. A bearded old man, straw hat pushed back on his head, reading an American Yiddish paper in the park.

Shultish stood before Gutman's house. He went up the walk and knocked. Heard footsteps. Miriam's. The door swung open.

"Good morning, *Adon* Shultish. How are you today?"

"Just fine, Miriam. Getting stronger every day. Is Gutman in?"

"*Adon* Gutman is in the study. Working. Come in. Shall I tell him you are here?"

"No no no. Don't disturb him. Maybe he's working. Writing. I'll wait till he comes out."

Shultish, following Miriam, watched her lithe body, walking seemingly on air.

"Have you had breakfast?" she asked over her shoulder. "If not, I can quickly prepare something for you."

"That's very sweet of you. I fixed breakfast . . ."

"Oh.". She arched her brows. "You cook? I thought that with your wife gone you would eat in a restaurant."

"Oh no! I'm a pretty good cook. Anyway, I'm still watching my diet. Perhaps I'm more careful than I should be, but I still don't eat at restaurants."

"It pays to be careful, *Adon* Shultish. But at least a glass of tea?"

"All right, Miriam. If you don't mind. And a slice of lemon. That would be just fine."

He heard Miriam leaving. Looked the other way, out the window to the panorama, so as not to stare at her body as she walked. Why should he make her feel uncomfortable? Of course he would rather have looked at Miriam than out to sea, but the truth was that even while looking at the sea he saw Miriam. Not that her image was reflected in the glass through which he gazed at the sea, but her image in his mind was projected out to the horizon. Tiny steamships sailed there; hardly visible white smokestacks were like cigarettes puffing black wisps into the sky. How Mrs. Gutman permitted such a beautiful girl to remain in the house was beyond Shultish's understanding. Perhaps because Gutman was older and not very attractive—he had a large head sunk into high shoulders and a gloomy, heavily lined face. Or perhaps Gutman lacked even a good imagination. Yes, that probably accounted for it. He was not even man enough to see what a treasure he had in his own house. The situation was strange. At eight Mrs. Gutman went to teach, and Gutman—who had taught for many years but now worked at the municipal archives—did not leave for work till eleven. The maid was there all day. That meant that he was alone with her for three hours.

Shultish sensed someone standing in the doorway. The lady or the tiger. Expected to see Miriam, smiling as usual, coming to him with a little tea tray in hand. Instead, Gutman.

Shultish rose, hand outstretched. "Ah, Gutman, *yedidi.*"

"How are you, Shultish? Shall I get you something? A glass of tea perhaps?"

"Thank you, Miriam already asked me."

"So Miriam already asked you."

"A treasure. The perfect maid."

"Oh yes. Rivka certainly knows how to choose a girl."

"Tell me," Shultish whispered, "doesn't a pretty girl like that have any ambitions? Schooling? Some other career?"

"Shh!" Gutman whispered too. "She thinks she's at Haifa University."

Shultish stared at Gutman for a minute. Gutman's face was expressionless. Two long lines ran down to his chin on either side of his nose. Then a little line—naughty, wild, gradually exploding—came into his eyes, and he burst into laughter. His face, his jowls shook. Shultish looked at his watch: ten-forty. I'll have to remember the date, too. The day Gutman cracked a joke. Humorless Gutman. What got into him? The Fichman Prize does wonders for people. Under the spell of self-delusion that they actually deserved the prize, even dull-witted archivists suddenly become wits.

"A joke," Gutman confessed. "Just a joke. It's actually a variation on a Yiddish joke. From your America."

"My America?"

"Whose, then? Mine?"

"It's not yours. It's not mine. I just happen to live there," Shultish said. "I teach Hebrew in the Diaspora. It's necessary—"

"No matter. Would you like to hear it?"

"Why not?"

"Why not?" Gutman said. "I'll tell you why not. Maybe you've heard it before. Maybe you won't like it. There are a hundred reasons why not."

"You're really very humorous today, Gutman. I congratulate you. Now let's hear the joke."

"Well, it seems that—"

Miriam stood in the doorway.

"A glass of tea for *Adon* Shultish," she called.

"Thank you, Miriam."

"Come with me, Shultish. I want to show you something."

"Thank you very much, Miriam. Very sweet of you," Shultish said. Glass in hand, he followed Gutman.

Gutman closed the door to his study. Shultish looked up. So that's what he wanted to show me. On the wall above Gutman's desk was the Fichman Prize certificate, luxuriously matted and framed, and next to it a picture of the President of Israel awarding him the prize.

"Beautiful. Beautiful. First time it's up, right?"

"Eh! My wife convinced me we should have it framed. I did it for her."

"It should be framed. It should. No small thing."

"Es iz bei mir vert a shmektabik," Gutman said in Yiddish.

Shultish laughed. "Once somebody wins a major prize, he can afford to dismiss it lightly and say it's not even worth a pinch of snuff."

"I know how you feel, believe me, *yedidi.* But I'm sure your book will get a prize too. It must. It should. It will."

"Thank you. But why bring that up?"

"Well, actually, it's on your mind. As a writer, I can see what is on people's minds. You'll get a prize, never fear. I've heard your book, your name, being mentioned in the right circles."

"Really? Where?"

"I'm not at liberty to say. But there is hope."

Shultish drew a deep, an endless breath, then looked up to the framed certificate again. "Is that what you wanted to show me?"

"No. Who said I wanted to show you something?"

"Why, you did!" Shultish said indignantly. "As soon as Miriam came in with the tea you said—"

"Of course, of course." Gutman closed his eyes and nodded quickly. "But I didn't *mean* I wanted to show you something. I just wanted to take you in here to—"

"—show me your prize certificate and the framed picture," Shultish teased.

"No! Just to tell you the joke my joke was based on. Do you still want to hear it?"

Shultish picked up a book of folk tales from Gutman's desk. It was brand new; Gutman obviously had not yet read it. "Of course I do." He began leafing through the volume.

Gutman did not begin. After a minute's silence Shultish raised his eyes and saw Gutman staring down at the book. Shultish replaced it on the desk.

"I can read *and* listen, but never mind. All right, let's hear the joke."

"I don't know if I want to tell it now. You spoiled it."

"Gutman"—Shultish jumped up—"If you don't tell me that joke now I'm going to leave the house this minute—"

"All right, all right."

"—board a bus, go down to the Haifa City Hall, take the elevator to the archives section, and demolish you in front of all your colleagues."

Gutman breathed through his mouth. He stopped in surprise, not knowing whether to take Shultish seriously or not.

Shultish pointed an accusing finger at Gutman. "I'm going to expose you, Gutman. Ruin your reputation. In front of three dozen people who do the work that ten can do. I'm warning you. I'll announce to everyone that—that you have a sense of humor. Now let's hear that joke."

Gutman swallowed, laughed a bit falsely, then, seeing how pleased with himself Shultish was, smiled.

"Well, this is the story. It seems that in a Jewish restaurant in New York there was a Chinese waiter—you've probably heard this story, haven't you?"

"No."

"—a Chinese waiter who spoke to the customers in perfect Yiddish. People took this for granted for a while until one man asked the owner, 'Tell me, sir, how is it that this Chinaman speaks such an excellent Yiddish?' 'Shh!' the owner replied. 'He thinks he's learning English.' " Gutman laughed. "What's the matter, don't you think it's funny? You *have* heard it before."

"Yes, it is funny," Shultish said, "and no, I haven't heard it before. It is a very clever joke and shows something about New York society at a particular period."

"Oh, don't be such a pedant, Shultish. Laugh!"

"Your joke was better. Because it reflected a spontaneous situation which—"

"Oy," Gutman held his head. "Speaking of a sense of humor, which office do I go to to make an accusation against *you?* My Lord!" Gutman looked at his watch. "It's almost eleven. Naamani will kill me."

"The boss still hits you for coming late?"

Gutman grabbed his hat and ran to the door. "Now that, Shultish, was funny. I withdraw my accusation. Why was it funny? It was funny because it was spontaneous. I'll see you tomorrow at the same time."

"Maybe."

Shultish, at the door, watched Gutman run for the bus.

At the corner Gutman turned, shouted, "Pardon me! Not tomorrow. Tomorrow I'm meeting my colleagues from the Acco and Nahariya archives at nine. In Tel Aviv."

Shultish shut the door, feeling for a moment as if he lived here and Miriam were his maid. "I think I'll finish my tea," he said. Turned, bumped into Miriam. Excused himself by lightly touching her shoulders, a polite embrace. She did the same. As she had done to Gutman the day he surprised her on the street corner. "It's nothing, *Adon* Shultish. You left your tea on *Adon* Gutman's table. Untouched. Was it too sweet?"

Shultish removed—or had he removed them already?—his hands from her shoulders.

He drank the cold tea in Gutman's study. Sipped the image of Miriam's face which floated like a plastic picture upon the tea. The gears in him stirred once more, invisible gears locking, finally, into place. Gears of sunbeams and gold. In place now. That was she. There was no other. He was sure now. Now he knew. She was the one. Even without reading it.

The Yemenite girl.

In the distance I thought I saw something strange: the figure of a young camel. But the sand is deceptive, in desert and shore. What I thought to be a young camel straightened and stood; a man with a knapsack had been tying his shoes.

Then I remembered the Yemenite girl. At that moment, when my heart felt empty too, I realized that I knew her better than I thought. How can one miss a person one doesn't know? How can one find one's heart empty if the person hasn't filled some part of it? Hence the reverse must be true: I must have known her; she must have already filled some part of my heart. And if I did know her, from where did I know her? We surely did not work together; we had no friends in common. There were no other places I could remember where we might have met. But then I realized I had erred. There was a place where we had met. The place where all of us had gathered, the souls of Jews born and unborn, all present at the Revelation. What matter, then, that she had made her way through the desert and settled in Yemen and that I had trekked to Europe? All souls had met in Sinai; all Jews melt in Israel; and now I was meeting the Yemenite girl, whom I had gotten to know best the moment she wasn't there.

At home that evening Shultish removed the Bar-Nun set from the bookshelf and opened the volume containing "The Yemenite Girl." He read half the story, then began pacing around in the empty house. The rooms changed places quickly. Amazing how energetic he felt. Not tired at all. He must be recovering all his strength. The body, how remarkable it was! First it betrayed you by becoming ill, playing the will for a fool. For no matter how strong the will, how passionate the desire to be well, if you were ailing, the will was feckless. But once the same body that had betrayed the will was well again, one saw the body's remarkable strengths.

He felt a strange itch, pacing in the rooms. The feeling came occasionally when he was writing and was about to get the high feeling of creativity, yet felt too lazy to open up to it and sought excuses for postponing writing. Tying shoelaces. Sorting papers. Washing hands. Taking a drink. Removing a waste-paper basket. Counting postage stamps. Sharpening pencils. A metaphysical itch. The living room, kitchen, bedroom, balcony. Empty. Looking

66

for his wife, trying to figure out why he was walking back and forth. Reading "The Yemenite Girl" did not suffice. A vacuum of disappointment roamed like hunger through his body. Something wasn't there that should be. It was like yearning for iced tea on a hot hamsin day and then only taking one sip. A song half heard. A quartet through earmuffs. A meal half eaten with appetite still strong. A girl swimming on the unreachable side of a pool. What other metaphors could come to mind? he thought as the rooms revolved before him. Who was moving, he or the rooms? Once a certain rhythm was achieved, it almost seemed as if he stood rooted and the rooms were pacing back and forth, the walls turning about-face in front of him. But Bar-Nun sat immobile at his table. Everything spun. Shultish glanced at the book, now closer, now farther away, once to his left, once to his right. He knew what he needed now. Bar-Nun's voice to accompany the story. The recording of "The Yemenite Girl" which he did not yet possess but heard clearly in the recording chamber of his mind.

Shultish sat and read the story again, trying to imitate Bar-Nun's Russian-Viennese accent. The figure of the heroine appeared more clearly than ever. No longer a literary re-creation, the mind's trick in turning words to flesh; now she was becoming real, assuming muscles, skin, face, like the resurrected in Ezekiel's prophecy. Like God into the clay Adam, Shultish had breathed *neshama*— soul—into the girl. Reading it, he clearly saw the heroine of Bar-Nun's "Yemenite Girl."

Miriam.

I used the flat rocks of the sea as my writing table and considered how I could approach her. I thought of this and that, and all the thoughts turned to water and slipped through my fingers. But I did not just go up to her. I got to know her the following way. Occasionally I would nod to her and she would smile back. We could have remained just nodding . . .

At nine-thirty the next morning he knocked on Gutman's door, waited to hear the familiar footsteps.

"Good morning, Miriam."

"Good morning, *Adon* Shultish. Come in, please."

Shultish stepped into the house and heard the door shutting behind him.

"Is Gutman at home?"

"He had a special meeting in Tel Aviv today."

"Oh, too bad." Shultish feigned surprise and took a step back.

"But you're welcome to rest here anyway," Miriam said.

"Why, do I look tired?"

Miriam reflected a moment. "No," she said slowly. "But you must have taken a long walk, and it is good to rest before continuing. Shall I make you some tea?"

Nodding, Shultish entered and sank onto the sofa. "Thank you, Miriam. That would be very nice indeed. With lemon, please."

This time Shultish did not look away, but watched her walking to the kitchen. First her legs moving across the Persian rug, then her hips, and then all of her until the door got in the way. She was not hunched over as other young maids were, as if the stigma of being a servant weighed on their necks and spines like a yoke. Miriam held her head high, as though the fruit-filled basket her grandmother carried on her head from the village market near San'a were on her head too. Shultish nodded to himself. Yes, he decided, Miriam was the one. Perfect for the part.

"I didn't put in sugar or lemon or anything. Here it is, all on the tray. Choose what you like."

"Thank you. You're very kind, Miriam. Really very kind."

"It's nothing, *Adon* Shultish. No need to thank me."

"Wait a minute, Miriam. Don't run off. I want to talk to you."

"The kitchen," she said self-consciously. "Work."

"Sit down, Miriam," he said, a little more firmly than he intended.

She sat, stiffly, at the edge of the chair, as though about to be scolded. A mistress in the States might have imposed a uniform on her maid, but Miriam wore what she pleased and ate at the table with the Gutmans. The democracy of Israel.

"Did you go to school, Miriam?"

"Yes, I finished two years of high school. But then I had to go to work, for it was hard on the family. Father could not afford it. High school is expensive here, you know."

Miriam said no more. She looked at Shultish and then, uncomfortable, gazed down at the rug. He too followed the interlocking floral pattern, the harmony of colors. He could lose himself in the endless continuity, the static perpetual motion. The secret of life, was it there? He too said nothing, worried if perhaps he had made a mistake in engaging her in conversation. The girl felt ill at ease. As Shultish was about to rise and depart, Miriam broke into a laugh.

"But I liked school."

"Would you go back?"

She settled into the chair, more relaxed now. She held her chin; a wise look passed over her face.

"I can't say. I know that everyone says yes. But I can't say yes so lightly. When I say yes I want to really mean it . . ."

The nuance of the words, their other-meaning, disturbed Shultish.

"Why do you ask?" said Miriam.

"Oh, perhaps because I teach. I like to see people in school. Do you like to read?"

"Very much. I read what *Adon* Gutman gives me."

"Would you like to read . . . something I wrote?"

"Yes, I would."

"You're not just saying it?"

"No. I will read it. Really. Bring it. But not tomorrow—" She smiled suddenly.

"Why not tomorrow?" he asked.

"Wednesday is my day off. Wednesday I go down to the beach, and the sea does not prompt one to read."

"So you like the seashore?"

"I love the sea and the seashore. That's the desert in me"—she laughed—"yearning for the sea."

"Beautifully said. You speak like a writer, too. Where do you go?"

"The Haifa beach. Where else would I go?"

Shultish knew he would have to put another turn to the conversation to preserve its life. Otherwise he would have to rise and say good-bye. He stared down at the glass he was holding and had an idea. Pleased, he said to himself: So ideas are not dead after all.

"So you go swimming to forget about dishwashing and kitchen work and housecleaning."

"No. I don't mind it. *Adon* Gutman and his wife are very good to me. And anyway," she said, shrugging, "I do much of the same thing when I get home."

Of course you do, Shultish thought. How can a maid have a maid? Or a slave a slave?

"To help your mother?" Shultish probed.

"How did you know?"

"I'm a writer. I can read thoughts."

Miriam quickly clapped her hands over her eyes, forehead, cheeks, not knowing which to cover first. "No," she said, frightened. "I'm not thinking of anything now."

"I'm joking, Miriam. It was only a guess. Of course you have to help your mother."

"You're really joking? You really can't look into my head?"

"Of course not. Obviously your mother has her hands full."

"There are seven of us. So there's usually something for me to do. For me to do," she repeated and jumped up. "Excuse me, *Adon* Shultish . . . I have to do the marketing."

No, he thought, I am not an old man. He stepped lightly, beaming, delighted with his visit. Bar-Nun, Bar-Nun is an old man.

. . . acquaintances, as I am with the man down the street whom I greet daily but if not for the mailbox on his gate would not even know his name. Then the simplest thing occurred. She went to bathe and returned shining wet, like a mermaid emerged from the sea; but then, as I was going to the water, just as our paths crossed, she stumbled. The Lord had placed a stumbling block in her way for me. She stumbled, and I rose.

It had been a long time since Shultish had heard the ocean from up close. From his window in the Carmel he saw that it had substance, but he had forgotten its other attributes: sound, smell, texture. The rush of the waves, their colors and rhythm, made him stop in amazement. Was it that long since he had been to the sea? How different it was up close. From afar it was like a picture postcard, a mechanical reproduction of something beautiful. But from up close—ah, from up close it was the difference between a woman in a photograph and a woman on the other side of the room.

The heat had not yet reached its full intensity. A cool breeze came out of the sea, bringing scents of salt and fish, and mermaids in cologne. He walked to the water, not directly from entrance to beach, but diagonally, to cover as much sand as possible. He had expected noise, but the beach was quiet. Not the hum and roar of a busy day on a New York beach. He could make out isolated conversations and hear the repeated smashing of the surf. As the tide swept back he went down to the wet sand and, playful, began to walk on his heels. They made little halos in the sand. White halos. Momentary halos. Disappearing as soon as they formed. Halos like the light on Moses's face at the descent from Sinai. Rays of light, which others turned to marble. He walked. It was pleasant in the wet sand; on the dry sand his feet made squeaking noises, like the cry of gulls. Shultish felt healthy. Now and then he glanced to left and right, casually, as if looking for a friend. Of course it was all an innocent flirtation. How could it be otherwise? He was fifty and she only eighteen or twenty. Of course he didn't look fifty; well, maybe he *did* look fifty after his illness, but he certainly did not feel fifty. Still, he was older, and married as well. With his wife in Switzerland he had almost forgotten he was married, but that was life and this was literature. Nevertheless, it was pleasant to think of Miriam—as heroine of Bar-Nun's story. And to talk to her—as reincarnation of the heroine. He could no longer think of the story without her, as a child who has seen a biblical movie always sees the starring actor whenever he reads about the biblical hero.

Music came from a portable radio. Bach. A suite with a flute solo. Shultish hummed along. As ordered as the sea. Predictable rhythms. Magnificent secrets. Each cluster of notes reminded of

71

encounters past. Yes, there were secrets. But he could talk to no one in his circle about music. His colleagues were indifferent to it. He doubted if Gotthelf or Millman ever went to a concert. Not to mention Shimshovitz, who would probably sooner go to Israel than to a concert. And he'd been going for nearly fifty years. If in some future interview someone should ask him what his favorite composition was, he would undoubtedly say Beethoven's Ninth Symphony or the Quartets. Or if it was a very prestigious publication, perhaps the Flute Sonatas of Bach. But in truth, ah yes, the secret—Gottschalk's *Cakewalk!* It stirred him; alone, he marched, strutted, waved his hands, leaped to its captivating rhythms, felt a keen sense of loss at not having been a ballet dancer. Oh, for the chance to leap like Nijinsky out on stage at the drum roll of that syncopated *Tarantelle!* He had once seen himself, out of breath, heart pumping, eyes shining in the mirror, after a private command performance. Yes, the *Cakewalk* was the greatest piece of music ever written. But he would never say that, not even to the interviewer who sought the unusual. And not even because Gottschalk was a Jew, or at least half a Jew, on his father's side.

Shultish watched a gull circling slowly. The waves came high, hesitated, then dropped with force. Bach was quicker. A fine counterpoint, the slow, ordered sea and the quick Bach. The slow gull; the flute a bird of erudite steel. And the mermaids peeking out of the sea, the mask of the half fish bodies discarded. Floating in all their nakedness. They too had orderly voices; with their reedy voices they sang Bach. The waves built up slowly, slowly, reached a height, and then, with a sigh, released their curved energy, plummeting.

"*Adon* Shultish! *Adon* Shultish!"

He closed his eyes to see if he was dreaming. He repeated the sounds to himself. From the dunes of Rishon she was coming. To him.

"*Adon* Shultish!" The voice approached, feet quick on the sand, and someone—what a light, pleasant touch!—tapped his forearm. "*Shalom, Adon* Shultish. You are here too?"

He opened his eyes. She was wet. Coming from the sea.

72

Strange, he had imagined her coming from her perch on the dunes. Now she was the mermaid coming from the sea, one of the mermaids who sang Bach with reedy voices, while that powerful drum roll syncopated from the Gottschalk *Tarantelle.* Her body was shining. Drops of water stood on her shoulders and chest, as though congealed. He saw the goose pimples. She wore a two-piece bikini. Her waist was like the pinch in the letter *Aleph.* He looked away from her nakedness. He could have encircled her waist with two thumbs and two middle fingers. She shook her head; a spray of water fell on his chest.

"Yes, Miriam, I am here. What a lovely surprise! I decided to come down to the sea today. First time in months."

"Isn't it beautiful?"

If he said yes and looked straight at her, she might misinterpret his words. He looked to the sea. "The Mediterranean is lovely. It is one of the loveliest"—he lingered on the word, savored its sweet and salty taste—"seas in the world."

"Have you settled down anywhere yet?"

"Not yet. I just came," he said slowly, wondering whether to sit with her. Of course you'll sit with her, he thought. Narrator must sit with heroine. That's the way it was written.

"Then sit with me . . . that is, if you don't mind."

"I won't be disturbing you? . . . I mean—"

"Oh no." She laughed, bringing her hands together. "I'm with no one. Come."

He looked into her eyes, brown and deep, then looked away.

"Thank you. Are you sure?"

"Of course. Now I know that you can't really see into my head."

Your father won't mind, he didn't say.

My father, she said.

Your father. You told me that you father doesn't like you to associate with—

"What is it, *Adon* Shultish?"

"Nothing, Miriam. I just stopped because I had a thought. An idea . . ."

"Ah," she teased, *"Adon* writer at work. . . . Here, this is my bit of sand. What are you thinking of? A book?"

Shultish sat down, cross-legged. "Not a book. I'm thinking of a story. In fact I've just gotten the idea for it."

"How wonderful! What sort of story is it?"

"Well, I've just gotten the idea. I can't really talk about it until I have some of it down on paper. But I will tell you about it. I will, Miriam."

Shultish lay back on the sand, feeling the sun on his body. Although his eyes were closed, he felt the young girl watching him, and it pleased him. When one closes one's eyes and looks down at oneself, age goes away. Maybe her eyes looked at him differently, too, and did not see him as fifty with graying hair. Maybe she only saw his face, wiped away the years, and was impressed with his barrel chest and hairy arms, back, and legs. He thought of the spot on his forearm where she had touched him, focusing on it like an X ray, recalling her fingers. Eyes closed, he saw the sunspots dancing in spectrum colors on the insides of his lids, remembering the moment when her fingers, still cold from the sea, touched his arm. Like a drink of ice water after hours in the Negev desert. Thinking of her touch made him want to be touched again. But then he would have to leave and come to the beach again and look for her and she would have to see him from behind and come up to him and grasp his forearms with her cold fingers and say, "*Adon* Shultish!" There had been a happy note in her voice; she was glad to see him. All her fingers, thumb too, all cold from the sea—how long did the touch last? five seconds, ten?—had touched and pressed his arm. But if he were to leave again and return, what if during this replay he did not find her? Or what if he saw her first? Would he go up and touch her arm with his fingers and say, "Miriam"? Would he do that? Here on the beach? Where people knew him and might wonder what he was doing on the Haifa beach with a Yemenite girl? When his wife was off in Switzerland caring for an ailing sister? After tending a sick husband for weeks in Haifa, the poor woman rushes off to Switzerland to her sister, and immediately her husband, not even fully healthy yet, is seen on the beach with a pretty bikinied woman young enough to be his daughter. That's a man for you. That's the thanks women get. But most people he knew were working now. They would not be on the beach in the morning. But there were some civil servants like Gutman, who was frequently at an out-of-town conference, a euphemism for a morning at the beach. Now, he sensed, Miriam was not looking at him any longer; she was looking at the sea. He opened his eyes; right again. Prophetic gift that Bar-Nun did not want to know about. Miriam sat straight, absorbing the horizon, her arms embracing her knees. Can a twenty-year-old girl have such full breasts already? How much effort would it take to rise and take her by the hand and run to the water with her—as if he were her uncle, or an old friend? Amicably, pleasantly, with no other motive that would stir up suspicion. Or his blood.

Shultish moved in the sun. Felt the sun flooding his senses. Even through closed eyes he saw a sky of light, fire bright. His wife was with her sick sister in Lugano, and he, recuperating, was with a Yemenite girl. From a story. And he was thinking of a story, too. A man had a right to be inspired by life to create literature. He couldn't shut himself up in his library forever. Not after weeks in bed. But he was well now; everything was well. The sun was filling his being. Saucers of light were pressing his retinas. He was thinking of a story. The sun was in him. Lying in the sun. Holding, as he had once long ago, the sun in his hand. And Schubert penetrated. Like a Kabbalistic riddle. The illness expelled. His body healthy. Shultish happy. What more could one ask for? A story was growing in his mind, slowly—that's how a woman must feel during pregnancy—inspired by Miriam, the heroine of Bar-Nun's "The Yemenite Girl." His story, too, would be about a Yemenite girl, not titled "The Yemenite Girl" but perhaps—well, there was time for that. He had always wished he had written Bar-Nun's famous story, and the next closest thing to writing it was translating it; and now, not word for word, but image for subject, subject for image, he too would create, not copy, "The Yemenite Girl." In any case, it would be a spiritual variation on the beloved tale. How similar were the events, how fortuitous! He was like Bar-Nun, an Ashkenazi writer meeting a beautiful Yemenite girl on the beach, and her father objects to the match because he came from Ashkenaz and she from Yemen. Are my origins too lowly? Shultish asked Miriam's father. Did we not, together, hear the thunder and absorb the words spoken at the Revelation?

Shultish's thoughts wandered on. The words were set. Predetermined. All that mattered was who came along to give them shape, form, position. He was only the instrument to release them. Was the tale he was writing his own? he wondered. Or was it another's who had retrieved it from someone else? Or was he Bar-Nun, Bar-Nun subsumed into him, re-creating the beloved tale?

Some days later I learned that she indeed was a rich merchant's daughter, even though Yemenites are not usually merchants. That her father was rich I had gathered, for when she told me her family name I immediately recognized it; it was known in Israel, just as my kinsman's name was known in Europe. When I asked her if I might come to her house that evening, she shook her head and said, "My father."

The phone rang. The ringing of the phone always bore some promise. Friend. Invitation. With his wife at his side he was not worried about the phone ringing. Now that his wife was gone the ringing could be the portent of some sad news. A hijacked plane. His wife aboard. It had happened once before on a Swiss flight. It was not a wrong number. The phone rang until he answered it.

"Shultish! How are you?"

"Fine. Just fine."

The voice puzzled for a moment. Shultish searched swiftly through a catalog of faces to match voice to visage; then his heart bounded.

"*Adon* Bar-Nun! Welcome back! Oh, how good to hear from you! What a lovely surprise." He closed his eyes for a moment, savoring the phrase. "How was Europe?"

"Should I say Europe is excellent? You know my works. Europe is an ailing beast."

Shultish, abashed, understood the hint. "And you? How is your health?"

"Well, it could be better. I made a mistake. A big mistake. I let myself be talked into going. Next time I get the Nobel Prize I won't go abroad. It was too much for an old man like me, leaping over the cities . . ."

Shultish laughed. Bar-Nun had punned on the famous phrase from the Song of Songs, *"me-daleg al he-harim"* (leaping over the mountains), by saying *"me-daleg al he-arim."*

"But what can I do?" Bar-Nun went on. "I am a Canaanite slave to the publishers, so I must say yes."

"I read reports in all the newspapers about your receptions in Zurich, Rome, Paris, London."

"Really? Did they follow me around to all those places?"

"Of course, of course," Shultish said enthusiastically, happy for Bar-Nun's success. "I've saved the clippings. I can show them to you if you like."

"Don't trouble yourself, Shultish; the publishers keep careful files, and they'll very likely be sending the articles to me. And what of yourself? How is your health? Are you completely cured and well?"

"Completely cured, yes. And getting my strength back from day to day."

"Thank God for that. And how is your wife?"

"My wife is well. She told me you met on the plane."

"We had a pleasant talk. A visit to a sick sister in Switzerland, she said."

"Yes. My poor Shoshana. She had to go from tending one sick person to another."

"He who goes and tends the sick is worthy of the world to come, says the Midrash. A very great mitzvah. What is new from Switzerland? One of my sons is ambassador there, you know."

"Who doesn't know that Bar-Nun's son is an ambassador?"

"If your wife needs any help, I'm sure Avraham will be able to help her. She shouldn't hesitate to ask him."

"Thank you. She told me you offered her Avraham's help. She's fine—her sister, too, is improving. It's very kind of you."

"For an old friend like you, Shultish—"

"I'm so glad you called. A lovely surprise. I knew you'd come back a week ago, but I thought: why should I bother you? You're probably busy from the trip, getting things in order, writing down your impressions."

"Very considerate of you, Shultish. And the main thing is that you're well."

"I hope you too will regain your strength."

"It's all in the hands of heaven, Shultish."

A moment of uncomfortable silence followed. Shultish did not know whether to ask his favor now, or whether Bar-Nun was leading up to something. A little barometer in Shultish's chest was suddenly filled with bile. He breathed; bile rose.

"Well," they both said at once.

"*Adon* Bar-Nun. There's something I want to ask you, if you don't mind. Do you remember I once asked you to record for me 'The Yemenite Girl'?"

"Yes. I remember. My son-in-law reminded me that I had made a tape for my son, Moshe. I sent you to him."

"Yes."

"You didn't get it?"

"Well, the fact of the matter is that—" Shultish bit his tongue. He had vowed not to say a word of the incident with Bar-Nun's daughter-in-law, just to say that he was unable to get the tape. "I could not get it," he said slowly.

Bar-Nun, that clever man, evidently read the pitch of his voice. So he sees through the telephone like me.

"Aha, so it was she—*she* didn't want to give you the tape."

The bile rose again. Shultish recalled the entire scene. He in bed, his wife returning in tears. That's right! The words rushed, tumbled, straining at his lips. And *how* she didn't want to give it! You should have seen the treatment my wife received!

"Not to me, to my wife," Shultish corrected him. "I was ill, you remember. I made an appointment and sent my wife down."

"I should have warned you."

The welcome she gave her. It was inhuman. And your son— Shultish bit his lip again. He knew

"You see, *Adon* Bar-Nun. It was really a surprise. She—"
he should be
"You mean, my son's wife?" Bar-Nun asked.
careful.

Shultish pressed his front teeth down hard on his lower lip. Tasted a speck of blood. Was at the point of revealing the entire story. If he told—even gently—he could win the old man's favor and sympathy and dispose him to agreeing to record for him. But he restrained himself from speaking ill of the woman. A vow was a vow, even if it cost him the recording. To increase peace in the world, to increase peace among people was a sacred obligation. The reverse was iniquity. Oh, Lord, guard my tongue from speaking evil and my lips from saying guile. So went the thrice-daily prayer. He would not add to familial discord. Even if it cost him the tape.

"No, I mean *my* wife. For I thought she would bring it back. To make a long story short, the tape could not be found, and Shoshana returned empty-handed."

For a moment—seconds long, like breath held in—there was silence again. It was Bar-Nun's move now. Shultish waited.

"You know reading tires me. The old story. The weak heart."

"I know, *Adon* Bar-Nun. You once told me."

"Yes, I know I told you. And I'm still not feeling too strong from the trip . . ."

Shultish told himself, "Careful!" His instinct warned him again to withdraw. To follow the lead of Bar-Nun's argument and agree that he ought not to read now, ought to postpone it for some other time. In other words, to submit as usual. But instead, thinking of the touch on his arm, the lovely surprise of meeting the Yemenite girl, he said:

"You'll soon recoup your strength, *Adon* Bar-Nun. After all, the air of Israel—"

"The Midrash only says it makes one wise. It says nothing about making one strong."

"How are you feeling now?"

"Thank God, slightly better. . . . Well, if you insist."

79

"Adon Bar-Nun. You know, all during my illness 'The Yemenite Girl' was on my mind, and now that thank God I've recovered—" But then again, he almost said, reading does tire you, he almost said, about to defeat himself again at the point of near-triumph. But Shultish did not say what he was almost about to say. His teeth slipped into the groove already formed on his lips and bit down harder.

He heard Bar-Nun saying, "Well, if you've recovered, we should consider it a get-well present."

"You'll read slowly," Shultish said solicitously, his head dizzy with excitement. "So it won't tire you. With a tape recorder one can stop whenever one wishes." He laughed for no good reason. "It's not like reading on the radio, or before an audience. You can actually rest."

"When do you want to come?" Bar-Nun asked.

"Whenever you say. When is it—" No. He was not going to go through that routine again. He had learned something from his illness. "You just name the day and the hour. Today. Tomorrow. Whenever. It's up to you."

"All right. Yesterday."

Shultish laughed. "Excellent. That's a wonderful joke."

"It's not mine. Unlike other writers, I don't claim for myself the fruit of others' labors and genius. You know who I'm talking about."

"Of course. Firkovich."

"I'm not mentioning any names. I told this joke and another one to Gutman before I left."

"About the Chinese waiter who speaks Yiddish?"

"He told you?"

"Well, he told me the joke, but he didn't say you told it to him."

"See what I mean about claiming credit for the fruit of others' creativity? Well, it's nothing new with him. Moses wanted to bring the Jews out of Egypt. Gutman wants to bring them back. That's why he was punished with the Fichman Prize. Don't laugh. All prizes are a punishment."

"I hope you don't consider the Nobel Prize a punishment."

"The bigger the prize, the greater the punishment. The greater the sinner, the larger the prize."

Then I must be a saint, Shultish thought. A perfect saint.

"You see what hell it is to be dragged all over the world," Bar-Nun continued. "They wait till a man is old and gray and then they give him hell on earth. *Preis* in German is price. That's the price one has to pay. For what sins I've committed I do not know. Well, never mind, I was going to tell you the story."

"I'd like to hear it," Shultish said.

"It's a variation on a famous story. Under the czars, as you well know, Jews were not allowed to set foot in Moscow except with a special permit. This one Jew finally got a permit for twenty-four hours, but naturally he overstayed his permit. When a policeman spotted him and asked him when he arrived, he blurted out, 'Tomorrow.' "

"Excellent!" Shultish laughed. "An excellent story. It captures the psychology of the *galut* Jew under an oppressive regime perf—"

"You know what, Shultish, *yedidi.* Come tomorrow at four-thirty."

"Wond—"

"No," Bar-Nun said more distantly,

Shultish bent down to pick up his heart as it spiraled down his chest, across his back, around his hips, tying him tight on its way down. Punishment, he thought, for making the old man do what he did not want to do.

as if he were speaking to the mouthpiece a foot away, or checking something on a calendar, "Make it five," Bar-Nun said.

The bile barometer in Shultish's chest was about to gag him again. So it would begin after all. Bar-Nun would hold out the sugar candy and at the last minute snatch it away.

"All right," Shultish said hesitantly, fearing Bar-Nun's next move. The barometer contracted. The bile rose, embittering his tongue.

"Good, Shultish. Good-bye. At five then. I have to go now. There's someone at the door. Today I'm expecting Ben-Gurion. Now that he is retired, he has time for me."

Shultish, overjoyed, sat down to write. His search for immortality. The printed word gave one *tehiyat ha-metim,* resurrection. With every reader, in every library, bibliography, footnote, one's life was extended. Eternal life was in the printed word.

Shultish sat down to write. In Hebrew. In Israel. Not writing for a dead Hebrew journal published in New York. But living Hebrew fiction for Israel.

At night, the rooms of his apartment seemed to expand. Going from one room to another was like walking across a grand ballroom. Each step clicked loudly on the tile floors. He had not washed the floors since his wife's departure. No maid had set foot in the house. Miriam? Hmm, perhaps she— Not perhaps. She would be delighted. Even the view of Haifa Bay from his window seemed farther off. The lights of the ships and the pier—they could have been the lights of Lugano, no? Water joined place to place, and here he was at the edge of the water—he could almost reach out and touch it—and his wife at the shore of Lake Lugano. Perhaps walking on that lovely palm-lined corso that swathed the lake. Shultish looked down at his desk, the half-empty yellow paper. Writing brought the rooms back to a size his heart could manage. Writing shrank the rooms, enlarged his heart, severed his fear. Even if he had to go to the bathroom or to the kitchen for a drink he did not fear the footfalls on the tile floors; they were no longer lonely clicks on endless palatial marble floors.

Pen in hand, Shultish stared at the lined yellow paper, aware that he was about to write. But he had to push his pen, force it to move across the page, as if the pen were a barrow and the paper sand. What had Bar-Nun meant when he said that Moses wanted to bring the Jews out of Egypt and Gutman wanted to bring them back? What was the key? The symbol? Liberation and slavery. He pondered, uncovered, stripped layer from layer, finally concluded: He meant *nothing* by it. It was just one of those word plays he's fond of. Should he tell Bar-Nun that he was composing a story about him, or, rather about one of his heroines? Bar-Nun had never really discussed Shultish's own stories with him; Bar-Nun had once hinted that he acknowledged their existence, but he had never given one word of critical appraisal. If Shultish were to discuss his fiction with Bar-Nun he would be his equal to a degree—creative writer meeting creative writer. It would give him a different stance vis-a-vis the great author. No longer admirer looking up to Nobel Laureate. But he didn't even have a rough draft to show him; just an idea and a few pages. No, he decided, it would be better to keep it a secret for a while. A secret from Bar-Nun, that secretive man.

Those words made me want her all the more. Not only did I have to win her love, I also had to vanquish the father and his pride. Why had she said no to a visit to her home? Did her father not allow her to go out? Could it be because my skin was not honey and the whites of my eyes not milk? Would white skin like mine be anathema to him? My origins too lowly? A man like me, descended from noted Hasidim and men of valor, not good enough for his daughter because I came from Ashkenaz and he from Yemen? Had we not stood together side by side at Sinai? Had we not, together, heard the sound of the shofar increasing in strength from moment to moment? Had we not, together, heard the thunder, the mountaintops clashing, seen the sparks of lightning made by stone grating stone, and absorbed the words spoken at the Revelation?

I saw the Yemenite girl in the evenings. Not at her home or at the sidewalk café, but by the dunes I met her. In honor of our meeting, the tide withdrew and gave us room, sand and space more than we needed. She clung to me with fury, not thinking of her father. But her father, transparent as film, came between our embrace and made me think of him. Her embrace told me that she thought of now; mine tried to keep from her my thoughts of what would be.

Although the water kept a respectful distance, it still roared and rumbled. The sky turned the color of ripe plums. Sea gulls cried and dived for fish. The sun had set and left its afterglow on the

horizon, as if the Holy One Blessed Be He had smeared the dying
red sun along the length of the sky. The world was at peace.

"Your father," I said.

"No," she said softly. "Let us not talk about my father."

I looked into her eyes. Sometimes her eyes were blue, some-
times brown. They shifted colors, as the dunes shifted their shape.
Isn't it odd that something you own you cannot see—until some-
one else comes along to provide the light?

That night Shultish dreamed of a pool surrounded on three
sides by a ranch-style cedar house. From the board at the base of
the U he dived, churning through the water with the strength of a
man half his age. The water was sweet. Here no chlorine. Sweet
water, river sweet. He swam for a long time. Head out of water, he
looked for the far side of the pool. Then came the waves, the taste
of salt. Ocean spray, rhythms of the sea. The sea drew him farther
and farther, but he struggled against it, trying to keep the cedar
siding in sight, to get to the rim of the pool. Waves are supposed to
push you in, he thought, not pull you out. He kicked harder,
younger now. Something tangled around his foot. A green rope of
seaweed. Then he saw her ahead of him, pulling him farther and
farther. Holding the sea rope, the Yemenite girl. Not naked. In a
bathing suit this time. To whom his loyalty now? To her, or to
Miriam? No, he shouted, bring me back. He jackknifed into the
water, slipped the seaweed chain off his leg. Rode the crest of a
wave like a dolphin, then grasped the enameled rim of the pool.
His head knocked against the tiles and he touched the cedar wood
with his eyes. Miriam sat beside the pool, playing his tape recorder,
listening to "The Yemenite Girl." She stroked her legs, rubbing the
sun in. Absently, like a cat flicking its tail. He knew it was "The
Yemenite Girl," but he could not hear the words. The sounds
came, but they were broken, distorted, scrambled, as though
someone were interfering with the recording. The more he tried to
listen to Bar-Nun's voice, the more tricks the tape played. A
sentence came through. And then words backwards. Sentences
misplaced. Words without syntax, like a dictionary list, and in

unalphabetical order. Or every other line skipped. It reminded him of a call he had once made. He had to get an address; the person at the other end kept repeating the numbers, but he could not interpret the sounds properly. Or perhaps *that* had been a dream? Miriam played with the knobs, but nothing happened. Then the Yemenite girl emerged with a splash from the sea and sat crosslegged, watching Shultish and Miriam. How alike they were. Like twins. Twins Shultish could tell apart. And list the differences. He looked again—now he could not. But one difference was always there. Miriam had wrinkles around her eyes from the real sun of Israel, while the Yemenite girl did not.

"Do you remember me?" Shultish asked the Yemenite girl. Miriam raised her eyebrows in surprise, but Shultish turned to the Yemenite girl. She smiled, then closed her lips, and then said, "My father."

Shultish was puzzled. "I asked if you remembered me." He glanced momentarily at Miriam. "I didn't say anything about your father."

"Let us not talk about my father," the Yemenite girl said softly.

Who was speaking? The Yemenite girl who sat cross-legged at the edge of the pool, her back to the shapeless sea that brought its salt waves into the pool? Or was it Miriam? Or was neither of them speaking, but only the tape?

"Don't you hear what I'm saying? Why are you talking about your father? Perhaps the waves are too loud." A fright came over Shultish. His words were not words. He was talking to the wind. Just as he could not hear clearly the words that Bar-Nun was saying in his tape recorder, so he could not make himself heard to the Yemenite girl. And Miriam—why did she sit there without saying a word? Could she not make herself heard either? Was she aware that the Yemenite girl looked so much like her? Was that perhaps the reason for her silence?

"Why are you talking about your father?"

"My father cannot see very well."

"We sit here watching the sea entering the pool, and all this Yemenite girl can talk about is her father."

85

"One can become a Jew," the Yemenite girl said, laughing, "but one cannot become a Yemenite. An impossible conversion."

"An interesting idea. I never thought about that," Miriam said.

"Tell us more about it," said Shultish.

"And leave my father?" the Yemenite girl said. "My father. My father. Let us not talk about my father."

"Don't you hear me?" Shultish shouted. "The waves are too loud. The sea is conquering the pool. The salt the sweetness."

"Do you want me to tone the waves down?" Miriam asked, fingers poised over the tape recorder. Shultish looked at her mouth and eyes to see if she was joking.

Shultish woke up in a sweat. He sat up in the dark, feeling very much alone. His head, still in the dream, was traveling as fast as a plane from the land of dreams to his bed. He felt the buzzing sound of flight in his ears, a sensation of quick displacement. The night was moonless. Gradually he made out the window and a ship's light in the sea. His eyes grew accustomed to the darkness, which brought some light into the room. He switched on the lamp, fully awake, in bed, in Haifa. But the light cut at his eyes like whip blows, and he put it out. He sipped at a glass of water on the night table and wiped the perspiration from his forehead and upper lip. He looked at his watch. Three A.M. The very heart of the heart of night. Throughout his illness, knowing, wishing, willing he would get well, he had not thought of death; now that he was well he had begun to think of it. Death did not come fluttering with black wings. It was an absence of movement, a cessation of being. Not skull and crossbones. He sipped more water, gripped the night table, rooted himself to room, house, Haifa, Israel, this world. He had seen what death was. Death was a paralysis of freedom, of will, movement, speech. Death was speaking the same lines again and again; the Yemenite girl destined for eternity never to think or articulate, but repeat and repeat the few phrases that she was given to say. Like a record stuck in one place; or even like a record itself. Freedom with circumscribed limits.

Death was being immured in a short story.

"And you?" I said.

Her eyes looked into mine and gave them light to see. "I have my own mind—can't you see?" she said.

"What would your father say if he knew?"

Yemenite girls are gentle and gracious. But mine, in addition, had a resolute mind. "We will not talk about my father now. He is of a different generation." And then she gestured to sand and sea. "But I was born here."

"And hasn't he already chosen a husband for you?"

The Yemenite girl did not reply. Was it the question that made her blush and become even more beautiful at that moment, or was it the truth behind the question? She laughed silently. Scoffing at whom? Or what?

Awaking in the morning, Shultish looked for the tape on his night table. Realized he hadn't received it yet. Yesterday he had had to wait until tomorrow to see Bar-Nun and get the tape. But now it was already today. His sleep, his dream, had changed a distant tomorrow to a reachable today. He remembered his nephew, the son he had never had, once saying as a child, "Today is tomorrow's yesterday." Why had Shoshana told Gershoni that they had no children? It was none of his business. He shook his head in disbelief. A Hebrew writer with a Christmas tree! If only it were known—but he couldn't say a word. "We'll leave it to our nephew." He had asked Shoshana later about her remark and she said, "I was just responding to his irony with some of my own. You never knew he had married a shiksa?" No, he had not known. It was literature that interested him, he told her, not gossip. So their nephew would get Gershoni's autograph, just as he'd get everything. But Shultish wasn't the only writer who had no children. Peretz had none. Bialik had none. Mendele had none. Moses Mendelssohn had three daughters, but look what became of them. All converted. In the Middle Ages the great Ibn Tibbon had three daughters, but he was only a translator. Then Shultish recalled that Rashi too had three daughters. The famous French commentator on Bible and Talmud was also an interpreter of someone *else*'s work. He too studied and analyzed and commented upon words. A smile spread over Shultish's face. The joy of discovery. Rashi. *Ezra Shultish.* With a simple Hebraic reordering of letters, quite common in Midrashic commentary, his name bore the letters of Rashi's name. Verbal trick or reincarnation? Coincidence or sign?

Shultish dressed, ate, and went out to talk to Gutman. On his way up the gently winding Herzl Street to Gutman's house, Shultish passed a barbershop. So early and so crowded? What holiday eve was it? Three men with scissors in hand were working in balletlike synchronization on the heads of three seated men. Shultish took nine or ten steps with the picture window of the barbershop floating along with him before realizing that he had seen a familiar face. Yarkoni, the writer, without a skullcap. Without a skullcap Yarkoni looked naked. He's the sort who wears his yarmulke while getting his hair cut, while showering, while bathing, while swimming. What is he doing in Haifa? Has a Haifa haircut suddenly become so chic in the eyes of Tel Avivers? Well, Yarkoni—in Berlin he had been called Teich, so naturally in Israel he shed that German river and became a Hebrew river: Yarkoni—had to improve *some*thing. His writing hadn't improved. At sixty the old translator was still trying to get his Hebrew stories published. Language made no difference to Yarkoni, Shultish wrote in praise of him in his thoughts; he was equally incompetent in Hebrew, Yiddish, and German. His one claim to fame in original literature was a memoir in Hebrew about Bialik which had been translated into English. Yarkoni also fancied himself a translator of Bar-Nun, since his one translation—"The Yemenite Girl"—had appeared in a Swiss-German anthology of Israeli stories.

Shultish stopped, returned to the barbershop. The barbers appraised him in their usual manner, staring first at his hair, then at the rest of him. Shultish felt ill at ease. His hair was embarrassingly short, cut the other day by a barber down the block. "No, no," he told them, and pointed to Yarkoni, who still had not seen him.

"Yarkoni, what are you doing here?" And he added in Yiddish

so that the North African barbers would not understand, "You think haircuts are cheaper in Haifa?"

Yarkoni gazed at him in the mirror. "Shultish! What a surprise! How are you feeling?"

"Better and better, Yarkoni. What brings you here?"

"We'll talk in a minute. He's almost finished." Yarkoni gestured to a seat.

Shultish sat down.

"Sit down, *adoni*, quite all right," the barbers said. "Here we're all friends. Long hair and short. Shaven and unshaven."

That was two questions Yarkoni hadn't answered. Why was he being so secretive? A bus roared by on the street. Shultish watched the number five until it was cut off by the window. Yarkoni eyed it apprehensively for a moment, then stared down at his hair-covered sheet. Ah, so that's it, Shultish realized. The number five went up to Bar-Nun's house. Yarkoni was going to visit him and had stopped in here to get his head cleaned up before meeting the old man. Yarkoni had probably proposed another translation into German, and Bar-Nun had acquiesced. Or perhaps Bar-Nun had invited him up with a proposal of his own, perhaps a book-length manuscript.

"Thank you," the barber said. "Next."

Shultish rose. Yarkoni placed his skullcap on his head and opened the door.

"What time is your appointment with Bar-Nun?"

"Ten-thirty," Yarkoni said, automatically turning his wrist, and then looked into Shultish's eyes in bewilderment. "He told you?"

"He didn't tell me a thing. I'm not his confidant. How is the book coming along?"

"So he did tell you. And it was supposed to be a secret. That man can't keep a secret."

"I told you he didn't tell me. I just figured it out. . . . Here's your bus."

Yarkoni made no move to board it. "It's early," he said morosely. "There's just no confidence any longer. . . . Tell me, why?"

"Stop being a child, Yarkoni. You're behaving like a prima donna. You think it's so hard to put two and two together. You live in Tel Aviv, right? So what are you doing on Herzl Street, which is the bus route to Bar-Nun? And didn't you translate 'The Yemenite Girl' into German? And why would you be getting a haircut here all of a sudden? Because you forgot yesterday, and this morning it was too early when you left Tel Aviv. And this is the route of the number five bus up to the top of the Carmel."

"You should have been a detective story writer."

"I like Poe. I once translated 'The Gold Bug' for my class," Shultish said, laughing.

"Maybe I was going to visit Gutman?"

"Impossible. Then you wouldn't have bothered with a haircut. And furthermore, that's where I'm headed—and he may not even be at home at this hour. Sometimes he has meetings."

"Then why are you going there?"

"On the chance he's there. We have to take chances. Yarkoni. . . . I'll tell you what. Why should we squabble? You told me a bit of interesting news, so—"

"I didn't really tell—"

"—so I'll tell you something. I'm going to see Bar-Nun too. He's going to do me a special favor."

"Namely?"

Shultish looked at his watch. "It's ten-fifteen. Don't you think you should be going? Why do you have a morning appointment? He never sees anyone during his working hours."

"It's an important matter."

"Which book is it?"

Yarkoni fidgeted with his lapel, shifted his weight from left leg to right. Adjusted his skullcap. Bar-Nun was right. Yarkoni was a nudnik.

"Well, if you don't want to tell me you don't have to."

"What's the special favor he's doing for you?" Yarkoni asked.

"He's going to record a story."

"Bravo. That's a coup. Which one?"

Shultish brushed from his forehead a fly that wasn't there, then slowly scratched his cheek.

"How are the short stories coming?" Shultish asked.

Yarkoni beamed. "Fine. The editor of *Milot*—"

Shultish sniffed: a third-rate journal.

"—wrote me that he'd like to see more of my stories. And you?"

"I'm working on one now. Two have come out in New York recently. In *Bimot.*"

"Is that magazine still around?" Yarkoni smiled.

"Why? What's the matter?"

"It's a nineteenth-century journal. I thought it died in 1910. Try writing fiction for some living Israeli magazines."

"For your information, some of the best Hebrew writers in the world publish in it. Why don't you try submitting a story?"

"Did you ever get your English translation of 'The Yemenite Girl' published in New York?" Yarkoni asked.

"Did I show you that?"

"Of course. A rough draft. When I visited you in New York."

"No. It wasn't published. I sent it to a dozen magazines, and they all said no politely."

"Curious."

"And then a year later some young American-born *shmekl* who doesn't know the first thing about Hebrew, who obviously hasn't devoted his life to it—I had never even heard of him then—comes along and translates 'The Yemenite Girl' into English. I had a translation of that story before the kid was even born."

"So what if it was published?" Yarkoni said. "A good story can be translated and retranslated. My version of 'The Yemenite Girl' in German was about the third or fourth one. Still, for the definitive anthology of modern Israeli fiction in German, the Swiss publishers chose mine."

"Why do you work in German? Doesn't it have a moral repugnance? You're a religious man."

"But I work *from* a sacred tongue. Some of the holiness clings to it. Why don't you try sending your translation out?"

"No chance. I've been disappointed too long."

"Well, it seems people do know of your translating ability."

"Do they?"

"Well, some writers told me that Bar-Nun called them and asked about you."

My God, Shultish thought, he *does* want to appoint me his official translator.

"Has he spoken to you, too?"

"I can't say. That is, I—"

"*Won't* say. Very nice."

"It's not that."

"Then what is it? Look, personally I don't care. I'll find out from him soon enough if he wants me. I thought I'd like to know just a little bit sooner."

"Wants you for what?" Yarkoni asked.

"What has he been talking to you about?"

Yarkoni sighed. "You really press one, don't you? It's about your interest in translation and writing and literature."

"See?"

"Frankly, I don't see. I see my bus. I'll have to take this one. And look, please don't mention anything to Bar-Nun about what we discussed earlier—you know—"

"Of course, Yarkoni, and you don't discuss with him the—"

Yarkoni boarded the bus.

"I understand perfectly, Shultish. When it comes to keeping a confidence, Yarkoni can be depended upon to be *sha-shtil!*" He put one hand to his lips and with the other waved good-bye from the bus. "Not like other writers," he said from the window.

Shultish walked up the street and stopped to rest by a bench. Thank God, forty-five minutes had already passed. Only five and a half more hours. He would spend an hour or so at Gutman's and then walk back to his house. Lunch and a short nap and he would be on his way back to Bar-Nun for the recording of "The Yemenite Girl."

"*Adon* Shultish! *Adon* Shultish!" A girl's voice behind him. He heard the sea, the crunch of feet on sand, waves breaking and breaking. Miriam, he thought. He turned and saw her holding two

92

large paper bags, looking exactly as she had in his dream. Did she know that he had seen her in his dream? Could she feel that special aura of intimacy that surrounded her because she had come to him in his bed in his dreams?

"*Shalom,* Miriam. Here, let me have a bundle," he said, placing both hands on one of the grocery-filled bags.

"No, no." She pulled away. His hand grazed her breast: soft, springy. His fingers tingled. "You've been sick," she said. "I can carry them myself."

"No, let me help you. I was just on the way over to see Gutman anyway." He remembered his wish on the beach the other day. In reaction to her touching his arm, he would rise, take her hand, and go to the water. He put his hands on the bundle. The left hand around the top, the right hand on the bottom as though embracing it. She resisted, and his hand pressed against her breast again. This time she did not turn away, and instead of grazing her breast his hand now pressed deeper into her flesh. A mermaid rose from the ocean, naked to the waist, a salt song on her lips.

"No, *Adon* Shultish," she said, seemingly oblivious. "Don't! Let me!"

Shultish felt himself blushing. "Who told you I was sick? I am well. Perfectly healthy."

Another mermaid rose, and then another. A trio, linked by seaweed, naked in the sun.

"*Adon* Gutman told me."

Mermaids don't live in the dunes. They live, naked, in the sea. Their voices are like the sounds of reeds. Lightheaded— embracing bag or Miriam?—struggling to get his syntax right, he said, "Does he . . . did he . . . everything—tell you?"

"No, not everything. But he told me you were sick."

Still helping Miriam. Miriam, by not moving, helping, burning him.

The wave came. The fourth side of the pool appeared. A rectangle now, shutting out the sea. "Here, let me have that bag," he said, his throat dry, his eyes wet with the sea.

Miriam turned away, perkily, flirtatiously, moving her hands up, grasping the bag, like a girl in a folk dance, miming harvest or a basket full of fruit: ripe cantaloupes, grapefruits, clusters of firm, juicy grapes. The movement of a girl being courted. She held the bag out of reach. Shultish dropped his hands. Her face beamed with laughter.

Harvest, harvest, harvest, Shultish thought.

"Do you think I'm so old I can't help . . . I can't help a young lady with her bundles?"

"Not at all. In fact you look very good. I saw on the beach how good you looked."

"Then why don't you give me a bundle?"

"Okay," she said in English. He stretched out his hand and took the bag carefully, avoiding another embrace.

At the house Miriam gave Shultish the key and asked him to open the door. Gutman had already left, she said. Within, a warmth moved from his loins and spread like a leaf, dark green and hot, to his chest and throat. The heat pressed like a vise, pounded at the sides of his cheeks. He placed the bundle on the kitchen table.

"A glass of tea, *Adon* Shultish?"

In the small kitchen he sensed it. She radiated heat, a sign she was ready. Shultish, middle-aged man though he was, had a young memory. He recognized it at once and responded on the same wavelength. He knew that these signals were often onetime chemical reactions, turned off if not responded to. Nevertheless, he did not remain standing next to her, he did not help her with the bundles or bump into her by removing the groceries item by item from the bag.

He sat down. Alone with Miriam, the Yemenite girl. She had given him the key to open the door. Excitement still encompassed him. The afterglow on his horizon; the sun smeared red along his sky. He had his hand on his knee, the hand that had touched the flesh of the Yemenite girl of his dreams. Don't call me *Adon* Shultish, he thought, rehearsing to say it aloud. He said it aloud in his thoughts, weighing the possibilities. But by saying that, something would change. Saying these words would involve some commitment. Don't call me *Adon* Shultish: he tested the words again. Then what would his next step be? At this moment his wife was probably calling the El Al office in Lugano preparing for the trip back to him. He looked at Miriam. She swiftly put the groceries away, folded the bags to be used for garbage. He did the same at home. His wife, too. In his mind, tea was boiling, steaming. The heat in the room, in his mind, from crown to toe, was unbearable.

Shultish rose, put his arms around her. She looked up, not surprised at all. As though she'd been expecting this. She turned her lips up to him. He felt her fingers at the back of his neck, grazing his hair, weaving in his hair. Her kisses tasted of salt, as if the sea had not yet been washed away. He kissed her, thinking of her not as a woman but as a friend, relative, an innocent kiss on the lips. He kissed her, but he still retained his marriage. In kissing her he did not forget Shoshana, who at this moment was riding the *funiculare* to the business section, passing Barton's kosher candy factory, on her way to the El Al office and home to him. He saw her; she did not see him.

Shultish rose, put his arms around her. Surprised, she leaped away as though stung. *"Adon* Shultish!" she said.

But he could not tell whether it was anger or a flirtatious refusal. "I just—"

"Adon Shultish," she said, withdrawing to the sink, as though seeking the protection of something firm.

"It's because I'm older than you, right?" he said, red in the face, embarrassed, hoping he could wipe away this humiliation, erase it like a tape. Hoping that she would say yes.

"It's not that. What is there between us, *Adon* Shultish? I don't see—" And she began to shake her head.

He did not know whether she was going to cry. "I'm sorry." He backed away. Could one draw a curtain and shut out the deed? How could he reverse time on what he had done? Erase the tape? Destroy the film? Wake up? "Don't say anything about this. Please," he mumbled, retreating to the door.

"I said would you like a glass of tea?" Miriam asked, holding the glass in her hands.

"Oh, yes, yes, Miriam, of course. Sorry, I didn't hear you. Thank you."

Calm again, he sipped the hot tea, sensing a different warmth now. He wiped his forehead with his handkerchief. The tea burned his tongue and throat, but it did not disturb him. He breathed deeply, pleased. He had not destroyed his world after all.

"What else did Gutman tell you about me?"

"You think all he does is speak about you?"

A sabra, Shultish thought. Definitely a sabra. Only someone born in Israel would come back with a remark like that.

"You were born here, right?"

"Well, not here in Haifa. But if you mean in Israel, yes."

"I'm sure *Adon* Gutman has many other things to talk about than me. I'm not foolish enough to believe—"

"I didn't say you were foolish, God forbid."

He looked for sarcasm on her face; none there. Stopped her with an outstretched hand "—that a man like him talks only of me. Nor is he foolish enough to do that."

Miriam looked to the floor.

Shultish saw the expression on her face. I've hurt her, he thought. I've hurt her. But she hurt me too. Was that retort of hers necessary? Shultish stirred the spoon in the empty glass. My remark was not nearly so sharp as hers.

"I just asked what else Gutman said about me. I really didn't mean anything else. I'm sorry if you—"

"He also told me you're a writer."

"Did he?" Shultish sang. That probably raised him in her estimation. For her a writer would be endowed with a halo of mystery that a teacher did not have.

"Is it true that you are a writer who writes stories and books and not a writer who reads thoughts?"

He could have said: *Adon* Gutman would not lie. Or: If *Adon* Gutman said it, obviously it must be so. But then he would be challenging her again. She teased him with her sexuality, true; but he felt he should not substitute a barb where he dared not offer an embrace. And what would happen if she came to New York and he asked her to visit him at his house and she came, and in the presence of his wife he hugged her in a welcoming embrace as if

96

she were a niece or a friend of the family? Would that embrace be any different if it was done in the presence of his wife? Or was it the length of the embrace that counted?

"I *am* a writer of stories and books, Miriam. And since Gutman told you that, I'll tell you something about myself. Well, not really about myself, but something personal."

Shultish rose and placed the empty glass in the rack on the sink. He turned on the faucet. Miriam said, "Leave it, *Adon* Shultish."

Shultish turned. "Miriam, I'm writing a story about you."

The kitchen was small. She stood by the refrigerator. The wave of warmth coiled into him again. Heavy at the bottom and spiraling lightly, airily, to the top, exuding yes and now, and yes and now. Miriam jumped toward him joyfully and slapped both her palms lightly on his forearm.

How long were they resting there? Shultish wondered, not knowing how long he wondered. His head felt as though he had taken cough syrup: sleepy and disoriented. His mind split into various zones. Her palms on his forearm, anticipation on her face. Where was he? Yes! What was the timing? Now! Should he? Could he? Yes, now! Did it make any difference if he kissed her before she kissed him, or if he kissed her now, as she was about to? Were her hands glued to his skin? Or was it the perspiration coming from his forearms?

Shultish turned and, rinsing his glass, took a drink of water. The room: flames were in its walls. The tea had seared him. The Yemenite girl had placed a column of fire in him. She disoriented him with her presence. Not her fault, he said. I asked for it. What am I doing here? Wanting to eat my cake and have it too?

"Is it really about me?"

"Yes, to a degree. Do you like to read?"

"Yes. Is it a love story?"

"In a way."

"Who is it that falls in love with me?"

"Who says that anyone falls in love with you?" Shultish asked, smiling.

"Oh, I just thought . . ."

"I can't really say now. Wait. I don't really want to talk about it until I finish it."

"The other day you said you couldn't talk about it until you had some of it written down."

"True. But it doesn't have structure yet," Shultish said, purposely using the Anglicized form of the word in Hebrew to puzzle and impress her.

"Promise you'll let me read it."

Did she say "promise" or "promise me"? What is wrong with me, he thought, weighing every word? He liked the word "promise." It bore the grain of intimacy. Intimacy. It sent a wave of memory back along a channel of no-time. Memory was timeless. It took time and placed it in a special zone. A cubicle sealed shut to the advance of ordinary time. Various memories floated freely now, overlapping. His mother reading Yiddish stories to him. The room, the day, the weather, when he received word that his first short story was published. First meeting in Vienna with Bar-Nun. First meeting with the Yemenite girl. How old was a memory? Did the things he remembered about yesterday have a different color, a different texture from the memories of childhood? His hands on her breasts were recorded. Her fingertips and palm on his forearm, that was recorded too. Only a moment ago, yet not brighter than childhood memories. Ezra, two or three, on Yom Kippur, under the table in the warm, narrow Hasidic shul, hot and bright with many glasses of burning wax. Or his grandfather's remark—the old man had lived to be one hundred and eight, so there was hope for him, too—that was repeated like a legend so often he believed he had heard it. At ninety-five he complained of discomfort in his right arm. The doctor, apologetic, ascribed it to old age. And *Zeyde* saying, "But my left arm feels perfectly fine and it's just as old." This too had happened only yesterday; it was not seen through the far end of a telescope. Not brittle or chipped or faded. Memory box was three-dimensional. Not subject to clock's erosion.

The question or me? A husband has been chosen for her, I

98

decided. But her kisses belied that thought and chased that suspicion. Her lips were sweet; honey was under her tongue; the fire of Yemen was in her heart and her love.

On the land, by the sea, under twilight and sky, when pomegranates and columns of marble seared our thoughts, we postponed the words that harbor deep in one's soul and which we fear will surface.

Shultish sat at his desk trying to write his story. Chin propped on his palm, elbow on the glass-topped table, he looked at the pages. The items on his desk blocked his thoughts, like scattered glass in a driveway, sawhorses on a thoroughfare. A little lamp with a shiny base. The smooth glass of the desk. A red soft-tipped pen. Some colored ball-point pens for rewriting. But what good was rewriting if first writing hadn't been completed? He looked down. There too was a Shultish holding a pen, elbow to elbow, with a puzzled look, gazing up to the real Shultish, who envied the glass image. But who was the real Shultish? Who really should envy whom? Shultish glanced at his watch. What a perfect time. Midway between his visit to Miriam and Bar-Nun's recording of "The Yemenite Girl," he sat at his desk with his own version of "The Yemenite Girl," which he was creating word by word. Sweating over thought by thought. If he closed his eyes he could see all the Yemenite girls blending, fusing their identity. The pen leaped into Shultish's hands. Now he would definitely begin. Then he jumped up. Remembered. The tape recorder. Batteries. Tape. What good was that magic moment if the mechanics of the recording were faulty?

"Testing, one, two, three. Ladies and gentlemen, 'The Yemenite Girl,' by Yehiel Bar-Nun, recorded in the house of the Nobel Prize winner by . . ."

He flicked the switch, reversed the tape, heard his words again. Batteries strong. Technology was working. He erased the sentence, set the tape with a few inches of leader.

Shultish looked at his watch again. Not too much longer. At the phone. If only it would not ring. Now he could think of nothing to write. Instead, he wrote the morning's events with Miriam. But his hand and pen did not move. Because the events were so different from Bar-Nun's story, how could they fit into the pattern of "The Yemenite Girl"? Perhaps the best thing would be to copy Bar-Nun's story word for word. That would be writing, too, wouldn't it?

What to do now? Shultish stood, walked to the window, and looked toward the sea. Perhaps this time Bar-Nun would invite him up to the library to see all of Israel from the window. There was only one recourse: simply to request it. Bar-Nun would not, could not possibly, refuse him. Irritated he might be; grumble to himself or later to others, perhaps; but refuse he would not. On the other hand, by recording for him, Bar-Nun was doing him an important favor, a historic favor, something he would never do for anyone else. He had not even told anyone, except Yarkoni. But it really wasn't Yarkoni's business. He had wanted to tell the good news to Gutman; instead he had paid a visit to Miriam.

The sea came and retreated. Shultish played his favorite game: unfocusing his eyes, transported to the distance. The window was clear. The Mediterranean chrome, hardly a dent in it. Ships skimmed over the metal sea. He looked for mermaids, but they could not surface, could not penetrate the sea chrome.

Shultish placed the tape recorder on the step next to the door and rang the bell. He was not nervous until the bell sound stopped. His heartbeat rose from his chest, to his throat, to the roof of his mouth. He heard the footsteps, perhaps a little slower than usual. A shuffle, as if Bar-Nun were dragging his feet in slippers. The door opened. Bar-Nun stepped out.

"Shultish, *yedidi,* how are you?"

"Just fine. Good to see you. How are you feeling, *adoni?*"

Shultish stretched out one hand; Bar-Nun put out two, confusing him for a moment. Should he too stretch out both hands and grasp Bar-Nun's two hands in intimate greeting? Before he could decide, he felt Bar-Nun's arms on his shoulders, drawing him closer. The old man pressed his face to his and kissed him on both cheeks. Still surprised, Shultish managed to graze his lips against

Bar-Nun's smoothly shaven cheeks. The old man's green eyes seemed enormous for a moment—sly, gleaming, quick—as in an abstract painting. To what did he owe this honor, this sign of long friendship? Was Bar-Nun reckoning the fact that they had met more than three decades ago in Vienna, and now considering him an old friend? Or had the old man genuinely grown to like him; had he missed him during the weeks he hadn't visited? Or perhaps it was a welcome back to the land of the living after so long an illness?

Bar-Nun stepped back, still holding Shultish's shoulder at arm's length, and inspected his face.

"You're not looking bad, my dear. Rather well, in fact. Your face is somewhat pale, perhaps, and a bit drawn. But otherwise, thank God, you don't look bad at all. How much weight did you lose? Come, come inside; let's not stand here."

Bar-Nun stood aside and waved Shultish in. Shultish picked up the tape recorder and shook his head. "Oh no," he said, and put his arm on Bar-Nun's back, waving him in first. "No, *adoni,* I come after you."

"Well, I see you brought the thing." Bar-Nun stepped into the hallway. "Let's sit down. But first"—he pointed to a bottle of cognac and a plate of cookies on a little table—"let's make a *l'chayim.*" Bar-Nun poured two glasses.

"To your health, Shultish!"

"To yours, *Adon* Bar-Nun." Shultish was pleased. The old man had called him "my dear"— he was a member of the family now, embraced and kissed by kin.

"I could use it. Thank you." Bar-Nun whispered a blessing, drank, and gently smacked his lips. He inspected the machine.

"It's a special lightweight model," Shultish said. "It can record up to two hours."

Bar-Nun sighed, as if distressed that he might have to talk that long.

"How does this modern miracle work?"

"I'm going to place the microphone in front of you. Then I press the button and it records. Just read at your usual voice level. No need to raise your voice. It's a sensitive instrument. And whenever

101

you feel like stopping, just stop and I press this button, and then we can continue.''

''Button and flower!'' Bar-Nun said, meaning: How wonderful! punning on the phrase in Exodus which described the decorations on the Tabernacle's golden candelabrum.

The old writer had the book ready, open face-down to the proper page. He picked it up, read the title and began the story. Shultish could not believe himself that fortunate. Something would happen to stop the recording. A phone call. An important visitor. Shultish panicked. If Ben-Gurion had come the other day, perhaps President Shazar might come today. It would be nice to see Shazar again, but it would ruin the recording. Perhaps Shultish was dreaming. He would wake up and find that it had all been a cruel joke. His head spun for a moment. He listened for the door, for the phone. The phone. He looked to the phone. The phone was off the hook. A magnificent gesture. Very considerate of Bar-Nun. Who said the old man was sly and planned good deeds with an ironic twist in mind? It showed he was a true friend. With tact and feeling. Old World grace. Shultish watched the tape proudly. Bar-Nun was reading. The tape was turning, moving smoothly from one reel through the recording head to the other reel. It was not buckling or bunching up. The plug! And he's two pages into the story. Oh, God! He knew it couldn't go smoothly. Something had to go wrong. It was too good to be true. The things you want most badly never come true. They come only to tease. I forgot to plug it in. A hot flush swooped like a shell behind his ears. He raised his hand to stop Bar-Nun, then relaxed: Battery powered. Foolishness. How else could it be working? He listened to Bar-Nun. The old man read slowly; he seemed out of breath. Shultish's heart pinched. Perhaps he had taken advantage of a sick man. But perhaps it was just an act, to express his displeasure at recording. On the other hand, Bar-Nun read well. The drama of his story came out in his voice. But he wasn't following the text scrupulously. He skipped some connectives. Substituted synonyms. Once he used the mishnaic word for ''took'' instead of the biblical. Too bad Shultish's memory couldn't keep track of the changes. What a treasure it would have been! Then, happily: It's being recorded! All he would have to do was compare tape with text. There were at least a dozen changes already. Not only would he have a tape, he'd have a scholarly article as well: "Changes Between Printed and Oral Versions of Bar-Nun's 'The Yemenite Girl.'" An article, and then an appendix for future editions of his book. He knew already what Kaften would think upon seeing the title. Those young Americans had such foul mouths. "Printed" would become "Anal," and Kaften would have another joke. Or else he might say: Most people take an appendix out; Shultish puts one in. For a moment Bar-Nun lifted his eyes from the book and looked at Shultish as if to ask: Are you enjoying it? Shultish smiled and gestured to signify that it was fine. Remarkable, after all these years, that the story still enchanted him. Even though the heroine repeated the same words, as she did in his dream. There was, however, one change. Since his meeting with Miriam, "The Yemenite Girl" had an added dimension: Miriam. *She* was the Yemenite girl. And when Bar-Nun read:

I saw her nostrils, curved and chiseled in perfection—that cut of pride and daring—and then her well-formed mouth and eyes that spoke an ancient language I understood so well . . .

he saw Miriam and only Miriam. He no longer even remembered what image he had had of the Yemenite girl before he saw Miriam. Perhaps he had pictured her in Miriam's visage all along; perhaps it was destined that he meet the real Yemenite girl to support the one in his mind. Bar-Nun read on. Shultish watched the tape. A river past a landing. The web of life. Bar-Nun was telling him a story, the story of the Yemenite girl. Could he understand its meaning? Shultish suddenly had an idea, a twist of plot similar enough to Bar-Nun's story to keep the Bar-Nun spirit and yet different enough to make it original.

Shultish watched Bar-Nun reliving the tale. His eyebrows moved up and down. He narrowed his eyes. His fingers opened and closed in gesticulation. Shultish was glad to be with Bar-Nun, because at least now he could not be writing. If I can't be involved in immortalizing Bar-Nun, he thought, at least I'm instrumental in stopping him from writing, which is important too. Ladies and gentlemen, at this very moment the greatest living Hebrew writer, one of the foremost writers in the world, is not writing, is not creating, because Ezra Shultish is making him read one of his own stories. To be the agent in someone's creative life, whether for good or for ill, is a grand thing. That's one less story Shultish won't have the opportunity of translating. That's one less story Yarkoni will. And at the very moment Bar-Nun is doing me one favor, he is doing me another: keeping a rein on his greatness so as not to further overshadow the short-story writer Ezra Shultish.

Shultish looked to the stairs that led to the library. He was alone with Bar-Nun. He had what he wanted. The tape. Alone with Bar-Nun. No son-in-law. No visitors. No phone calls. Nevertheless, now was not the time to ask Bar-Nun to show him around upstairs. Enough was enough. There was time. The old man was tired. No doubt Bar-Nun would invite him again.

"Finished," Bar-Nun said.

Shultish flicked the switch off. "Thank you. Thank you very much, *Adon* Bar-Nun. Really, thank you very, very much. I have no words. I wish I could do, if only in part, for you what you've done for me. You've made me very happy."

You've made me very tired.

Shultish looked up. Had he heard that? Or was it an ironic ring in his own mind? An unvoiced but deserved rebuke?

He reversed the reel carefully and rewound the tape. Bar-Nun watched with interest, aloofly amused at the electronic device. Shultish replayed the first few sentences to show Bar-Nun how well it worked, then removed the tape from the recorder and placed it in a specially prepared, labeled box.

"Well, I hope I've satisfied you," Bar-Nun said.

"Thank you. You read magnificently. I'll put the machine in the corner by the doorway, if you don't mind, so it won't be in the way."

The old man looked down at his fingertips. The skin on his hands was pulled tight; little wrinkles ran over the skin—the only signs of old age on Bar-Nun.

"By the way, *Adon* Bar-Nun, what did you call the heroine?"

"Shultish, I'm surprised at you. Weren't you listening?"

"Of course, I—"

"I didn't give her a name."

Shultish laughed. "You misunderstand me, *Adon* Bar-Nun. I know that. And how I know that. I know your story so well I know it by heart. Don't you know how many times I've read it? Recited it? I wish all your readers were like me in knowing your stories. And *how* do I know this story! 'The Yemenite Girl,' for me, is like a beautiful piece of music that I know by heart."

Bar-Nun placed his hand on his heart.

God, no! Shultish thought. His heart. A spell of weakness because of the reading. Lord, no! Please, no! Bar-Nun bowed his head just as the characters in his stories did when they wished to thank someone. Then he looked up, no twinkle in his satiny green eyes.

"I don't like music," he said flatly.

"That I know, too."

"Music is a misuse of the human intellect. Emotional self-abuse. The deed of Onan. Fruitless intellection. Music stirs up the emotions the way a dictator stirs up a crowd, and offers them only temporary relief. Like an egg with the yolk sucked out. Empty shell. Music is like an aspirin. But words heal. Words teach. Words create. Words move. Words endure."

Not so, *Adon* Bar-Nun. Music speaks too. It tells more than words. Music becomes things, while words only represent things. Have you ever heard Gluck? Or Bach? Or the half-Jew, pure American, Gottschalk? Can't you see each note coming out in shape and form and touching you, bits of crystallized vibrating light?

"I'm sorry, *Adon* Bar-Nun. I just used music as a metaphor. In the sense that I know exactly what comes next. Of course I know your heroine has no name. I'm just wondering if when you wrote it you thought of her as having a name. That is, if you had a name in mind."

Bar-Nun laughed. "Shultish, it's a good question. But you know, if I had a name for her I've forgotten it. A character is important to me only when I'm creating him. Once he's done I forget him. I have to make room for others. Let Langweil remember them."

"But Langweil is dead . . ."

"All critics are dead. They are dead as soon as they are born. No, no, *yedidi*. I don't mean you. *You* are a writer. . . . Do you know German, Shultish?"

The question caught him by surprise, but he said, "Yes, of course. Don't you remember Vienna, when I came to you as a youngster?"

"Poor Langweil is dead now. There was a rumor that he died while reading the proofs of an article he wrote about me."

"Yes, I heard that in New York."

"To quote the Bible: 'He was like his name.' Do you know what Langweil means?"

"Yes, boring. *Langweilig.*"

"Good. So you will understand. Langweil, *langweilig*. Like all his writings. Although I don't know music and I don't use its symbolism in my work, Doctor Langweil's writings are a symphony of yawns."

"But didn't you once tell someone who asked about the meaning of a story, 'Go to Dr. Langweil'? You said, 'When I wrote it, I knew and God knew. Now I've forgotten and God won't tell. There's only one person who knows my works better than I—Dr. Langweil. . . . Go to Dr. Langweil.' "

"Is that what I said?"

"Yes. That's what everyone says."

"Well, then I must have said it. *Vox populi*, *vox dei*. But now I don't know what I meant by that either. Maybe the visitor stayed too long and I wanted him to go to Dr. Langweil for a longer while. Maybe I was being sarcastic. Maybe I meant just the opposite. And maybe . . ." Bar-Nun narrowed his sparkling eyes. A laugh glimmered in the tiny wrinkles and in the moving pink cheeks. "Maybe I was joking. You do allow me a joke once in a while."

"Of course, *Adon* Bar-Nun. What a question! The comedy in your works is well documented."

"A future article, hah? 'The Comedy in Bar-Nun.' "

"Not everything is subject for an article. I am, despite my book on you, not really a critic. I am a creative writer. But of course if you wish me to write such a piece—"

"No, no. You do allow me a joke once in a while, don't you?"

Shultish laughed. "Of course, *Adon* Bar-Nun. What a question! The comedy in your works is well documented."

Bar-Nun laughed too. His green eyes lit up. "Wonderful, Shultish. You are one of the few people who can make me laugh. You and my books. Although some of our sages of blessed memory denigrate laughter, I think a sense of humor is necessary for a writer. Show me a writer without a sense of humor, and I'll show you a man who is not a writer."

Shultish broke into a hearty laugh, hoping that Bar-Nun indeed intended the remark as a joke, hoping that Bar-Nun was not insulting him.

"You see, some people understand me and don't quote me. Some quote me but don't understand me. I've also been quoted as saying that it's lucky we have Homer in Hebrew, because that means he is safe. That he will survive."

"Yes. I've heard that too. That's another one of your famous sayings. But sometimes people change it to Shakespeare, or Dante, or Heine, or Tolstoy. . . . Then, actually, you mean to say you didn't mean that?"

Bar-Nun placed his hand on Shultish's shoulder. "Shultish, *yedidi.*" He moved closer. "I can talk to you. You are a fellow writer. Who creates. *Ex nihilo.* You're not a *langweilig* scribbler who eats others' creations. It is *we* who feed them. You and I are not mosquitoes—so I can talk to you. The others I tell what they want to hear. But you are a *Hebrew* writer. One of us. I talk to you from the heart. Hebrew is no longer a holy language. It is not different anymore. They have made it as goyish as all the others. I should return to Yiddish, but it's too late. Yiddish at least is ours. So you know who is really safe?"

"Who?" Shultish asked mechanically.

"Shakespeare is safe. He's in English. Tolstoy is safe. He's in English. Heine is safe."

"Then you're safe too."

"Of course. Have you been translated into English, *yedidi?*"

Shultish did a little jig with his head, saying yes and no. "Well, in a small magazine, the *Judaic Review.*"

"Excellent. Then you're safe too. Your writing will be preserved. Who is your translator? Is he good?"

Shultish swallowed. "I myself."

Bar-Nun laughed. "Then he must be good. Ah, Shultish, Shultish. Don't be embarrassed. The greatest writers have brought themselves into other languages. The very founders of modern Hebrew literature, Mendele and Peretz, did it from Yiddish to Hebrew. Even Sholom Aleichem wanted to do it, but he never had the time. Conrad translated himself from Polish to English, Tolstoy from Russian to French, Knut Hamsen from Norwegian to German. You're in good company. Why even I, had I known English, would have trusted no one else. Even Kafka intended . . ."

"Kafka? I thought you never read Kafka."

The chartreuse green, the green illuminated from within, of Bar-Nun's eyes went dark. Bar-Nun said through tight lips: "Not only have I not read him, I have never even heard of him. . . . But we were talking about Moshe Langweil, weren't we? I don't suppose you know what he died of, do you, Shultish?"

"No. I don't know what it was. Was it a stroke?"

Bar-Nun looked earnest, but Shultish thought he could detect a tremulous laugh in the eyes behind his eyes. "It wasn't a stroke that killed him, my dear. It was his own writing. Which is why so many critics die at their desks. Langweil, in fact, was bored to death."

Shultish boarded the bus, elated. He had not felt so wonderful in years. He had felt like this when he published his first short story;

and when at a Zionist meeting in his youth he found that the girl his eyes sought out liked him too, and later married him. And when he had his name in the *Times*. Shultish felt at peace with the world. He leaned his elbow on the metal ridge of the open window. No pain. Heard the birds in the trees as the bus moved along. The ones here continued the song begun by the birds he had left behind. Each man under his vine and fig tree. The messianic dream. The sea moved like a dream sea in an oil painting, brighter, closer, rocking, rocking. Not Bach, not Gluck, but that magnificent drum roll of the Gottschalk *Tarantelle* came back to him. He felt like dancing. Bar-Nun recorded for me. He pressed the tape recorder closer. And for my students. So when I teach it, I can—that is, they can have the pleasure of listening to the author himself reading the story just for them.

The bus ride back made him dizzy. Bar-Nun's words and the hairpin curves. Dizzy, yes—but jubilant. Bar-Nun and Shultish: writers. But what kind of writer was he? A Jewish writer? An American? Hebrew? Israeli? Perhaps Israeli, since his book was published in Israel too. In fact, he was more Israeli than the ones who lived here. Me, he thought, I'm the *real* Israeli. For he certainly wasn't American: he knew nothing about baseball. There was a time when, like a European intellectual, he had looked down his nose at the American sport, and considered it just so much foolishness. Like an East European yeshiva student, he had never held a ball in his hand.

One day, at the Hebrew Teachers Academy, one of the youngsters in the high school department, a thirteen-year-old, came running into the hall shouting: "Reiser got four homers . . . seven RBIs." Shultish couldn't comprehend the boy's excitement. Between classes he pulled over a colleague, Gotthelf, who had been in the United States for years and spoke almost without an accent.

"Gotthelf, I want to ask you something in private."

Gotthelf beamed. He looked as if he expected to be treated to some delicious gossip. He tried to press down the corners of his lips, which were trembling in anticipation.

"Of course, Shultish. What is it?"

Shultish spoke softly. "What's an RBI?"

Gotthelf rubbed his cheek. "RBI? . . . R . . . B . . . I . . . ?"

"Yes, that's it. Do you know?"

"Maybe . . . a kind of medical test. Like a GI series?"

"I don't know . . ."

Gotthelf stepped back, as if suddenly realizing that Shultish might be contagious. At arm's length he jabbed a finger into Shultish's chest. "You?"

"No," Shultish said, irritated.

"Is it Mrs. Metkopf? She hasn't looked good lately. Her typing, frankly, is going downhill."

"No, no, why medical?"

"A union, perhaps? Like AFL or CIO?"

"Can a man have seven of them?"

Gotthelf moved closer, held Shultish by the lapels, and asked closely, unafraid now, nose to cheek: "Who do you know who has an RBI?"

"No one. One of the students came running in and said that one of the boys got seven RBIs and four homers today."

"Homers!" Gotthelf began to laugh. "Homers!"

Shultish's eyes lit up.

Gotthelf saw that Shultish had finally understood. "Now do you realize?"

"Of course," Shultish said. "One of the boys must have gotten four copies of *The Odyssey* for his Bar Mitzvah, and to him it's an excitement. Four Homers."

Gotthelf leaned his head back and clapped his hands. "Oh, Shultish, you half-baked American. It's baseball slang. A home run. The player got four of them."

"All right, all right. Don't look so happy at my expense. Then what's an RBI?"

Gotthelf stuck out two index fingers. "Now *that* I don't know. It's baseball too, but I can't tell you. I only have a master's degree. For that you need a Ph.D."

The bus stopped. Passengers were getting off. His stop. Just in time. He picked up his tape recorder, cradled it like a baby in his arms.

Shultish stepped off the bus, smiling. The smile was reflected within, too. An image of an image. Deep inside him there was a series of Shultishes, smiling, mirrors to infinity. He stepped into the apartment as if it were a new dream house, enjoying every line of the furniture and every room, matching carpet to sofa and sofa to drapes, curve of lamp to pillow, sheen of tiles to books. He framed everything he set eyes on and made a still-life of it. Placing the tape recorder on the table, Shultish thought: Shoshana should be here at this moment. He raised the flap of the case to draw out the historic tape. And found his hand touching leather and air.

Quickly he groped. Touched. Tapped and felt. He groped the case. Touched every corner. Felt all his pockets, hoping. Back pocket. Shirt pockets. Touched the inside of the leather case with his right hand, while touching, tapping with his left. Praying that what he hadn't found the first time he would find the second. Retraced his steps through the living room, no longer framed but a space to get through. Went across to the front door, to the hall downstairs, outside, immersed in noise—leashed, unleashed dogs barking at his ankles; bus horns, motorcycles, exhaust fumes—of the street, to the bus stop. Held on to lamppost as he bent over, dizzy, in his search. Nothing. Only cigarette wrappers, gum wrappers, yes, here in Israel too, old bits of street debris. Ran back, heart beating, bursting, to the house. All the writers gathered in his living room. He was panic-stricken, ashamed. He would have to tell them, Gentlemen, I don't have the tape. The reporters would say that his voice broke, that he made the announcement with tears in his eyes, his voice choking with emotion. Shultish gazed at the tape recorder until its edges frayed out of focus and disengaged into two. Only half an hour ago it had contained the tape; now nothing. Was this death too? The nothingness that comes of something. Something suddenly nothing. Death had many pictures, many shapes. One death, a thousand faces. Like man, whose one life bore scores of simultaneous variations. Each with a different picture. Death was this: stumbling along in the twentieth century while one was royally entombed in the literature of the nineteenth. Writing for a magazine that died half a century ago. Like Gershoni. The Hebrew writer with a Christmas tree. Death was one's will tied eternally, immured in a short story. The paralysis that is death. Death was possessing for a moment the thing that eluded you, the thing you never thought you'd achieve, then stupidly losing it. Like the naked girl who beckons, then swims away through a net impenetrable only for you. Shultish stood next to the table, his head lowered, his arms dangling at his sides, conscious of the blood swelling in his wrists and fingers.

"We're shlimazels, Shoshana," he told his wife.

"You and me," she said.

"No," he decided. "Not you. Just me."

"It happened to me, too."

"But I *got* the recording, then lost it. What am I going to do now?"

"Call him up."

"No. Oh no. No, no. . . . And tell him I lost it?"

"Maybe it's there," his wife said.

"Then he'll call me. If I lost it there, obviously he'll call me."

Shultish retraced his steps mentally. How did he leave? Who sat next to him on the bus? Was it Firkovich? Perhaps it was Firkovich. Firkovich was the type who would do it. It had happened when he dozed off. Pickpocketed. He'll hold it for ransom. Firkovich the Karaite. Go start another schism, Gutman said. The Karaites, also dead, had killed off the joy of Jewishness centuries ago. Because the Torah said, Ye shall kindle no lights on the Sabbath, they sit in darkness. To light fires on the Eve of the Sabbath, to bring light into the house for Sabbath, that much sense they didn't have, those masochists. But still, there was something Jewish in them. Their stubborn streak. That's why some survived. Like Firkovich, the culture thief. No wonder Firkovich can't create. Signing one's name to ghost-written books wasn't creation. To create, one needs light. The Karaites have lived in darkness for a thousand years. No wonder they didn't survive. To survive one also needs light. Naturally it was Firkovich. Firkovich was just the type to lift a tape, or a manuscript. Yes, Firkovich took it. He'll ask me to write some articles or a book for him and then he'll give the tape back to me. I'll probably write him some book for which he'll win a prize.

Bar-Nun was absolutely right. Firkovich puts out books that no one wrote and no one reads.

The bus swerved. The clip was open, and out the little tape slipped. Or perhaps another pickpocket. Oh, God. He had felt a little halo of happiness, and now it had gone, halo turned to a stone wreath that pressed down on his skull. Sharp claws of pain moved slowly in his abdomen—hunger, perhaps. Perhaps the old familiar feeling of disappointment. He went to the refrigerator, removed a tomato and a triangle of cheese. With a knife he squashed the cheese down on a slice of bread, hastily chewed and swallowed it. He knew he shouldn't be eating so quickly but, while knowing, swallowed unchewed lumps of bread and cheese. Bit into the tomato which he forgot to salt. No time for boiling tea. He drank a glass of milk, beginning it in the kitchen, finishing in the hall. Jacket and hat from the closet—it was evening now, cool in upper Haifa—and ran to the bus stop.

Retrace your steps, he told himself, retrace your steps. He boarded the bus up the hill. Sat in the same seat, looked—hoping it might be the same bus: the ads were the same, exactly. Searched the—eyes of passengers roving on him—empty seats. Found nothing. He walked a jagged line to the front of the bus through ascents and sharp turns: stopped, resting till the bus stopped: up to the driver.

"Excuse me, how does one go about finding something lost on a bus?"

The driver did not turn his head. A careful driver. Dark face. Handsome profile. Too big for a Yemenite. No kin to Miriam. A Tunisian perhaps. Where did *he* get enough money to buy a share of the expensive bus cooperative? The driver took fare, checked the sides, obviously proud of his job, content with the ritual, shifted into gear.

"For example?" the driver said, still looking ahead.

"Does it depend on the item lost?" Shultish said with ironic singsong.

"Perishable or nonperishable. Dry goods or mechanical," the driver replied automatically.

113

Shultish saw four offices—aha, Israeli bureaucracy!—spread over the four corners of Haifa. Lines, repeated visits. Ricocheting from office to office.

"Perishable or nonperishable," the driver said again. "Dry goods or mechanical."

Shultish was aware now of a silence in the bus. He didn't turn, but saw people straining forward in their seats.

"Perishable and mechanical," Shultish said softly.

Now the driver turned and smiled a row of strong white North African teeth at him. A bite like a healthy colt.

"Hah? You're joking with me, *adoni*. What is it"—he raised his voice—"a mechanical apple, or a motorized cheesecake?"

Shultish heard laughter from those in the front. He knew it was funny on a superficial level, could even have analyzed why had he had the time and inclination. But now he didn't think it was funny.

The driver slowed down and, looking at the nearby passengers, shared his delight with them.

Shultish said, "I'm referring to a tape. Which is mechanical. And can be easily damaged. Hence perishable. Now do you understand?"

"In that case, I'm sorry. Why don't you call— Excuse me, a stop."

The driver braked, opened the door, called out a street.

"Hey, excuse *me*, my stop!" Shultish ran out.

"Adoni!" the driver yelled. "How—?"

"I'll call lost and found. Never mind," Shultish shouted at the shutting door.

"You're going to see Bar-Nun?" the driver leaned out the window. "In that case—"

But Shultish no longer heard. He walked up the street to the writer's house. To the very entrance, searching the ground, picking up objects. Rocks, clods of earth. Grass. Weeds. A dried goat turd. Lights went on and off in Bar-Nun's house. Through the row of fir trees that served as a hedge he saw Bar-Nun's figure, once here, once there. Was the old man watching him? Shultish hid behind a tree. He dared not be seen. All he needed now was to

114

have Bar-Nun discover that he had already lost the precious tape. He retraced his steps from Bar-Nun's house to the bus stop. He walked hunched over, looking. Ah, there it was. Heart leap up, Shultish down to the ground. To pick up a flat stone, deceptive at night. Like everything else he looked at. There a toy. An old bagel. Tonight, even footfalls had the shape of a little tape.

On the bus again, he half rose, about to ask the driver again— thank God it was a different one—but restrained himself. He marched up from the back, casually looking at the seats. Perhaps *this* was his bus. It had surely had time to make the run again. The passengers looked at him and he sat down, waiting for his stop. Obviously someone had picked his pocket. How else could it have disappeared? But why should anyone pickpocket the tape? What value did it have to anyone else, and who would even know he had it?

Shultish stepped off the bus, perspiring. He felt an odor of sweat and fear rising from his shirt. Although it was a cool, clear night, his back clung to his shirt as if it were a midsummer noon. From the bus stop to his house, nothing. Not even a stone to elate the senses for a moment.

Through the empty hall, filled only with the sound of his feet, and into his house, where he called Haifa's main bus station. "Lost and found, perishable and mechanical section."

The man at the other end laughed gently: "No, *adoni,* there is no such thing. Lost and found is lost and found. We have no subdivisions."

By his voice and accent Shultish could tell that he too was an Eastern Jew. He was smaller, less handsome than the driver. But more accommodating. He had dark eyes. A skullcap on his head. This one was very likely a Yemenite. Brother, cousin, kin to Miriam.

"But a bus driver, just minutes ago, told—"

"Making fun, *adoni,* a joke."

"But it's not a joke as far as I'm concerned. This is nothing to joke about. It's something very valuable. Something for *Adon* Bar-Nun. Lost."

"Ah, *adoni.* We'll do our best. Things lost on our buses turn up eighty-six percent of the time. We'll do our best to help you. What is it?"

"A little tape."

"Tape? You mean sticking tape? Like scotch tape?"

"No no. Tape for a tape recorder." My luck, Shultish thought, an Eastern Jew. "You know what a tape recorder is?"

"Of course, *adoni*. You say it was lost on the bus. At what time? What place? If you can tell us more or less, we can figure out which bus it's on."

Shultish scratched his head.

"Let's see. About five-thirty I boarded it up on the hill, at the crown of the Carmel."

"Just a minute." The man was humming, tapping his fingers on a chart. "That's Yossi's run. . . . All right, we'll have a look and call *Adon* Bar-Nun if we find it."

"No. God, no!" Shultish said in a fright. "Don't call him. It's a surprise. . . . No, no . . . and anyway, he's got an unlisted number. Call me, Ezra Shultish, at 46673 . . ."

"Yes, *adoni*. I'll call you tomorrow morning after the buses have been cleaned."

Shultish hung up, exhausted. It had been a long day. What now? A man is given the opportunity to touch greatness once in his lifetime. Finally he gets it, actually seizes the sun for an hour, then expunges it, extinguishes it of his own accord. Shultish, enervated, lay down in bed, saw nothing in the ceiling of his imagination before he fell asleep. Ruined. Opportunity lost forever. Another death. I can't ask the old man to do this again. Suppose he died? No, that's a terrible thought. A terrible thought. Enough death. Shultish turned on his side, crimped his leg. Felt uncomfortable. Tried to forget the terrible thought that his lips had made his mind utter. Perhaps it is in Bar-Nun's house after all. You're right, Shoshana. Perhaps it was kicked into some dark corner. But I can't call Bar-Nun and ask if he found it. Then he'll realize how lightly I cared for the precious object.

"You don't know what this means to me, *Adon* Bar-Nun," Shultish had told him afterwards. "It's like having a dream come true."

"Then you're a lucky man, Shultish. Because that's why they're called dreams. By its nature a dream is a distant wish, rarely coming true. So you've accomplished a rare thing, Shultish. A rare thing. A precious thing."

"What *you* gave *me* today is a precious thing, *Adon* Bar-Nun. What you did for me is a precious thing. I'll treasure this tape the rest of my life. Students will share it. It will be in their memories. Having heard Bar-Nun. It will be something to tell their children."

"You're a lucky man, Shultish. A lucky man."

A lucky man, Shultish thought. It was the last thing he heard from the darkening ceiling of his imagination before he fell asleep.

The next morning, not waiting for the call, he dialed the Egged Bus Company.

"Egged-Haifa, good morning."

"I'd like to have some information concerning—"

"Just a minute . . ."

Click, click.

"Transfer this to bus infor—"

"Wait. I'd—"

"Bus information. For what city, please?"

"For no city. I want information about lost and found."

"Either information *or* lost and found, *adoni!*" The girl had a bored voice. She too was North African, primping her hair as she spoke, looking at her fingernails. Dark honey-skinned, wide cheeked, miniskirted.

"People are waiting on line here." And to someone next to her said, "Listen to this. Some joker"—she tried to suppress a giggle—"wants information *about* lost and found."

"Don't be so impudent. Just connect me with lost and found."

Click, click.

"Give this party extension twenty-five."

"Hello. Lost and found."

"Ah, good morning. I called last night. Yes, I did lose something. And they told me to call this morning. A reel of tape from a tape recorder. In Yossi's bus. The late run."

"Yossi's bus. Yossi's bus. Wait a minute." The man held his

117

hand over the receiver and shouted. "Anything on Yossi's bus?" The place sounded like a cavern. Shultish heard the echoes, "Yossi's bus," bouncing back and forth. A windowless basement, probably. Huge, with lots of lockers in it. Lit by unshaded weak bulbs.

"Nothing?" the voice said, then turned to Shultish. "Nothing. They found nothing."

"Nothing? Nothing? I spoke to someone late last night. A Yemenite. A small man. With a skullcap."

"You mean Zion."

"Yes, that's him. Zion."

"They let you in? At night? How did you—?"

"No. On the phone. I just spoke to him on the phone."

"Then how could you tell what he looked like? You have television?"

"No, I'm a writer."

"And you see through the telephone? What color shirt am I wearing? Do I have a long nose or a short? Is my wife pregnant?"

He had a long nose—Shultish could tell that by the voice—but he wasn't going to get drawn into games like that. He'd had enough teasing from members of the Egged Bus Company.

Nevertheless, he couldn't resist saying, "Your wife is pregnant."

"Oh no!" the man said. "It's my fifth. And she'll be a girl, too. Do you think it will be a girl?"

"I'm not a fortuneteller. Just a writer."

"Oh yes, Zion mentioned something about Bar-Nun."

"Well, he's a writer, too. I was the one who lost it. Not he."

"Makes no difference who lost it. He shouldn't be ashamed to say if he did. We wouldn't find it any quicker. Or slower. But we didn't find it anyway. But don't despair, *adoni*. As sure as I have a pink shirt on and a long nose, I'm sure you'll find the tape. If you can see a skullcap over the phone, you'll find your tape too. Without lost and found."

The questions gnaw, like Scorpio, and never cease until they triumph.

"You'll have to come away with me, as Ruth followed Naomi."

"One can become a Jew," she said, laughing, *"but one cannot become a Yemenite. An impossible conversion."*

"Then you'll convert." I laughed in turn. *"You'll come away with me."*

"And leave my father?"

Shultish did not know how the next two—or was it three?—days passed. Looking at the calendar to see when his wife was coming home was one of his few amusements. He mesmerized the phone, incanting some salvation. Would it bring him news? Or would he have to make a call and discover for himself where the tape was? Shultish felt like the Jewish man—another Yiddish joke!—who had lost his glasses and looked for them everywhere except the top of his head. That he saved for the very last—his last resort. For if he did not find them there, in the hair above his forehead, they would *really* be lost. Shultish too. Calling Bar-Nun was *his* last resort. But life wasn't like the joke. If he called Bar-Nun, Bar-Nun would know. And he did not want Bar-Nun to know.

Even though he did not want to think about Bar-Nun, Bar-Nun thought about him. Communicated to him, even vicariously. Lying in bed before his afternoon nap, Shultish listened to the radio, hoping to distract himself. But again, Bar-Nun. Speaking through the Bar-Nun collector, Moshe Lichtenstein.

Lichtenstein had everything written by and about Yehiel Bar-Nun in Hebrew, as well as all the works that had appeared in translation. Lichtenstein was telling the interviewer how he had tracked down translations in far-off lands, corresponded with editors in Spain, Sweden, even in Japan, who kindly furnished him with copies. Then he told of the man himself.

"I had never met Bar-Nun, and naturally I wanted very much to meet the person whose work I was collecting. There comes a time when the literary and the personal seek to fuse. But I never wanted to impose upon his precious time. Incidentally, I should also add that I'm a typesetter by profession and I've typeset many of his stories—another thing that links me to Bar-Nun. One day I finally decided, yes, the time has come. I'm going to dare to try to see him. I knew he lived in Haifa, and since I was going to spend my vacation in the Carmel, I thought I would try to get in touch with him there. But I didn't know exactly where he lived. And anyway, I wanted to make sure it would be proper for me to ask to see him, especially now that he had won the Nobel Prize. I remembered that once in Haifa I had seen a picture, a very wonderful portrait of Bar-Nun, in one of the photographers' studios. I think his name was Weitzmann. The name stuck in my mind because Weitzmann was a famous children's photographer in Vienna, and one of my earliest portraits, age one, bears his imprint. In any case, I went to Weitzmann and discovered that he had indeed photographed Bar-Nun. I asked if I could buy one of the pictures, and he agreed. After I told him who I was, I asked his advice about seeing Bar-Nun. Weitzmann said that Bar-Nun was a wonderful man who received visitors kindly, but warned that he really did not like visitors, for they encroached upon his time. He gave me Bar-Nun's address and I wrote to him, telling him about my collection and about my lifelong dream to meet him personally. I promised not to take more than fifteen minutes of his time. I told him I was vacationing in Haifa and that he could either write to me or phone me at the hotel. The very next morning I got a call from him inviting me over the following day. He received me with open arms, as if he'd known me for years. Served me cognac and cookies and hovered over me like a favorite guest. Instead of fifteen minutes we talked for more than two hours. Before he spoke of anything else, he asked about me and my family, then entertained me with anecdotes about my home town, Lemberg. When I told him I had typeset his recent short story collection, *Ha-nahar Ha-yavesh* [The Dry River], he smiled, pulled out a new copy from a shelf, opened the book, and placed his finger into it to mark the place. 'God does wonders,' he said, 'but man can equal him. God splits the sea, but man can change a river into a fool.' Seeing that I was puzzled, he opened to page 142 and explained, 'See? You left out the *h* in "nahar" [river], which makes it read "naar," or fool in Yiddish.' I apologized. 'Never mind,' he said. 'You're an excellent typesetter.

Would that all writers had typesetters like you! One error in 430 pages? That's a miracle in itself.' I had brought a copy of that book with me and I asked him to inscribe it, for I had no autographed copies of his works. 'Ah, with pleasure,' he said, and took his pen and wrote on the flyleaf: 'To Moshe Lichtenberg, a typesetter with golden hands. May his tribe increase in Israel.' My heart fell. 'Dear *Adon* Bar-Nun,' I said. 'My name is Lichten*stein.*' Bar-Nun slapped his forehead. 'You see how divine justice works? I criticized you for a slip of the pen, and now God, who doles out measure for measure, has punished *me* with a slip of the pen. Please forgive me. I was thinking of the artist Moshe Lichtenberg, who just sent me some illustrations for one of my stories, and I became confused.' And do you know what Bar-Nun did? He went to another room and brought out a bundle of books and reprints. He autographed for me his two novels, the story collection *Ha-nahar Ha-yavesh,* and three reprints of recently published stories. That's the sort of man he is. It was one of the most memorable days of my life.''

Shultish, alone like a Bar-Nun hero, keeping house himself, Shoshana still away, took his medicinal walks, his recuperation strolls along the Haifa streets. Halfheartedly. The tape was gone, true. Still, he had his body to take care of. The will to walk was faltering; his legs were even less keen. Where previously he had enjoyed the sensation of a brisk walk—its pleasure, the feeling of healthy energy well expended—now he tired easily. His appetite flagged. A nasty sign. Was he falling ill again? With worry, his heart beat quicker. Listening to his quickened heartbeat, he was certain he was having a relapse. And each time it was the fault of Hebrew writers, Hebrew writing. Gershoni made me ill with his Christmas tree, and now Bar-Nun with his tape. If Shultish stopped his walks altogether, he would give in to invalidism and remain sickly the rest of his life. The doctor had prescribed walking, the best antibiotic. He had to get his muscles back to shape after so many weeks in bed. So he dragged his lukewarm will, he dragged legs outside. And pretended he enjoyed it.

121

A few days after the loss of the tape, he bumped into Gutman on Herzl Street.

"Why so sad, Shultish, *yedidi?* Where have you been? Is something wrong? How is your wife?"

Shultish stopped and looked Gutman in the eye. "With you the four questions are one. With me—four. I'll follow the precept in the Ethics of the Fathers and answer the first first and the last last. I'm sad because I lost something. I've been nowhere. Something is wrong. My wife is presumably fine."

"You're beginning to sound like a Bar-Nun character. That formal introduction to an answer! The analysis of a question. Read some other Hebrew writers. You're getting into a rut. What did you lose?"

"Don't laugh. Bar-Nun again. A tape. I was going to tell you, but you had left already. The tape Bar-Nun made for me. 'The Yemenite Girl.' The thing I've been dreaming of for years."

"Bar-Nun recorded? For you?"

"Yes. Why the surprise?"

"He never records for anyone."

"You told me that before. Still, he recorded for me."

"Did you tell him?"

"No, I didn't tell him. I sneaked the recorder into his house under my vest. Then out of the blue I asked if he could read 'The Yemenite Girl' without a mistake. Because I just happened to have a wild urge to hear it."

"What are you talking about?"

"A bitter little joke," Shultish said. "What are *you* talking about? What do you mean, did I *tell* him? You think I'm crazy? I *asked* him."

"Asked him *what?*" Gutman said, wrinkling his nose.

"To record for me."

"What are you *talking* about, Shultish? I asked if you told him you lost the tape. You know lately it's difficult to talk to you. You never understand what I'm saying."

"My very thoughts about you. *You're* hard to understand. You speak without transitions. Are you all right? Maybe you need an RBI test. It's a kind of medical test . . ."

Gutman glanced over Shultish's shoulder, as if seeing someone. He looked impatient. "Well, *did* you tell him?"

"No. I'm afraid to."

Gutman looked at his watch. "I'll tell you what . . . why didn't you come over?"

"I'll be glad to," Shultish replied, then realized that Gutman had phrased the question in the past tense. It wasn't an invitation. Now Gutman would surely think that he was losing his mind. Those damned transitions of his.

"First you come every day, and now suddenly you disappear."

"I wasn't in the mood."

Shultish looked past Gutman, saw Miriam floating in the distance. Above the park, between the trees. Her figure was vaguer than he'd thought it would be. She was transparent. Inside her a child walked along the stone ledge of the park. Again the tape. Since its loss, some spark had faded. He had no energy to think of his short story. Two and a half pages were done, another two in outline. The papers lay on the table like slabs of flat stone, heavy and dead. Shultish had no desire to continue writing. It reminded him of the lost tape. He had no desire to see Miriam. She reminded him of the lost tape. The tape was the link. Planning to have it gave him strength; having it in his possession raised him aloft; he levitated. With joy. Bursting with excessive strength. Now that it was gone, his Samson locks were suddenly shorn. With sudden clarity, through Miriam's transparent body, he realized why he had lost the tape. It was punishment. For expressing joy at wasting the master's creative time. While recording, Shultish was directly responsible for Bar-Nun not writing. Each man suffers, the sacred books stated, according to the extent of his sin. Measure for measure. That's why the tape was denied to him.

"And woman shall cleave unto her husband and leave her mother and father," I quoted.

123

We sat side by side, hunched into the sand, our hands hugging our knees, as if excluding others by that self-embrace.

Then a shadow crossed our line of vision.

"My father," she said.

The shadow approached, fell over the dunes.

The phone rang. My wife, he thought. The plane has landed.

"Hello," Shultish said.

"Shultish, *yedidi,* how are you?"

For a moment, perhaps no longer than an eyeblink, Shultish blanked out. He was aware of himself holding the receiver. I am holding the receiver, he told himself. Bar-Nun is calling me.

"You know who's calling, Shultish?"

"Of course, *Adon* Bar-Nun," he said, sensing the laughter in Bar-Nun's voice. Shultish's hopes suddenly rose. He's laughing because he has good news for me. "Of course I recognize your voice. Shouldn't I recognize your voice? How is your health?"

"Not bad. Did you notice something strange in the literary pages recently?"

"No, I can't say that I have."

"Well, it's just a bit of gossip. Gossip doesn't usually interest me, except when it connects with Hebrew literature."

"Anything interesting?" Shultish asked.

"Gossip is always interesting. But one needs self-control with it. Personally, I don't believe in gossip. But since you ask, I might as well tell you about it. No sense relating gossip to those who aren't thoroughly fascinated by it. . . . The news, you see—well it's not actually news, but I'm speculating—is that Gershoni is sick."

"Gershoni sick? Really? Wouldn't that have been in the papers?"

What am I doing. Shultish thought. The tape, the tape. Talking about one thing, the tape the tape, and thinking of tape tape tape another.

"I said I *supposed* he was sick."

"Why?"

"Ah! That's a good question. Because he finally published a short story."

"I don't understand," Shultish said impatiently. He looked at the receiver. Bar-Nun. The tape. Bar-Nun: Do you hear me? The tape. I want to hear about the lost tape, he shouted with the voice box of his mind.

"You see, Gershoni *must* be sick. Because all these sixty-seventy years that he's been healthy he hasn't published a word. Now that he's published a piece there must be something wrong. I presume a change in his physical state. Sick."

"Why, that *is* interesting news. Gershoni actually wrote a story. Did you read it?" On tape. Is it called "My Jewish Christmas Tree?" Taped. Tape box.

"Of course not. I don't read fiction by anyone over eighty. And to show you I don't mean anything personal, I'll reveal a secret. I don't even read the things *I* write. A principle is a principle. No exceptions."

"Do you read the younger writers?"

"No. I don't read anyone under eighty, either. Except you, of course, my dear. Because though I said I don't read anyone over eighty or anyone under eighty, I didn't say that I don't read writers who are exactly eighty. And you, my dear Shultish, I consider exactly eighty. So you I read. And furthermore, if I read, I wouldn't write. So if I have to choose between my reading what others have written and others reading what I've written, I prefer the latter. Not out of pride, of course. But duty."

"Of course," Shultish said dreamily. "Of tape."

"It is said of Gershoni that he was blessed with just so many words. Once his allotted number was up, and this occurred during a conversation decades ago, he merely stopped in mid-sentence. He could conclude only with a gesture. And to continue communicating in this world he had to repeat himself. Like a speech on a phonograph record whose vocabulary is limited and which only says the same thing again and again. And again and again."

"Perhaps I'll read it," Shultish said feebly.

"Look, *yedidi,*" Bar-Nun said. Shultish saw the words which he thought of as leaves now changing color and shape. They became sharper, like pine needles. "Look, Shultish," Bar-Nun said crisply, one key higher, finer pitched. "Did you by any chance lose the tape?"

"Yes. Who told you. Yarkoni?"

"What does Yarkoni have to do with it? I saw him *before* you came with that machine of yours. . . . Oh ho! Now I understand. Did he run to see you after he left me? Did he talk? These pseudo writers can't be trusted with a thing."

"No, no. I didn't see him after his visit to you at all. He didn't tell me a thing. Not a word. I just got mixed up. I thought I saw him the morning after. But I bumped into him the morning before my afternoon visit to you."

"I don't understand, Shultish. You sound mixed up. In short, no one told me. I just found it. Here. By the door."

"Oh, thank God it's safe. You don't know what days I've gone through. So you have it. In your possession. At home."

"I have it. In my possession. At home. In my jacket pocket. The inside one. Next to my heart."

"Thank you for calling, *Adon* Bar-Nun. You saved my life."

"Why didn't you call me right away?"

"I didn't want to cause you anguish in case it wasn't there."

"It caused me no anguish at all," Bar-Nun said, "for it was here all along."

"But I didn't know that."

"You should have called and you would have known. You don't know how upset I was for you. I know how much you value this tape. You called it precious."

"But"—the words sprang out, as if snapped by a rubber band. Shultish watched them in their trajectory, could do nothing to bring them back. They flooded his mind like a sudden spray of light, the perfect thrust against Bar-Nun for stretching his suffering—"then why didn't you call me right away?"

You didn't find it right away, Shultish answered for Bar-Nun. Otherwise you would have notified me immediately.

126

"What?" Bar-Nun asked.

"I said, then why didn't you call me right away?"

"I didn't want to cause you anguish in case you found it some-where else."

"I don't understand. I don't understand." They're all alike. Bar-Nun, Gutman, Yarkoni, Gershoni. None of them knows what he's talking about. They sound like something out of a madman's diary.

"I mean, in case you hadn't found out yet that you had lost it. No sense worrying you sooner than I had to. Do you see?"

"I see."

"In other words, in case you didn't want to play it for a week. . . . Would you like to come to pick it up?"

"Why, of course I would."

"Or would you rather I mailed it to you?"

"I'd rather come to pick it up."

"It could be sent registered, you know. Then it wouldn't get lost again and I wouldn't have to trouble you."

"No trouble at all, *Adon* Bar-Nun."

"All right. If you insist. I'd like to see you anyway. And talk to you awhile."

"I'm glad, *Adon* Bar-Nun. . . . I've been thinking of something and I want to say it to you. Forgive me. I apologize for taking your precious time during that recording. I should have said it sooner. I took time away from your writing."

Bar-Nun laughed. "Don't be childish, Shultish. How can you take my time away? Men aren't gods. Only God can remove, reduce a mortal's time. And do you think writing is only with the pen? On paper? In seclusion? I thought you were a writer! You should know. Writing is done in the most surprising times. Under the most unusual circumstances. While sleeping. Or talking. Even while recording."

Another bus ride, Shultish thought. He hoped the driver—mechanical apple, motorized cheesecake—wouldn't recognize him. He averted his face. The same driver going on the same route. Destination, Bar-Nun. Always the same journey, always a different purpose. He looked out the window. My life is a journey—to Bar-Nun. He caught the frame of the window in the periphery of his vision. Another picture hung on the wall. Colorful stage, propped with people and trees. There was Gutman's house. Miriam, he thought, and, as if by command, a vision of her floated in his mind. Then the real Miriam appeared, there on the street. Shultish's heart fell, burst like a bag of water. For him Miriam crumbled there on the street. Now she was a two-dimensional jigsaw figure, partly floating, disjointed. Too bad he had seen her. Now she was finished for him. No longer any hope. Even the tape was not so desirable now. Miriam was walking down the street hand in hand with a soldier. From her left hand dangled a green plastic shopping basket. Hand in swinging hand with a soldier. Her brother? Impossible. One doesn't walk that way with one's own brother. He turned, following her with his head, eyes, whatever, but the bus curved around and up the slope and she disappeared. For a moment he saw only the boy and the two clasped palms. Like a snapshot poorly composed. Shultish looked down at his chest as though inspecting his heart. Seeing what? Disappointment? Jealousy? His heart beat quicker. A sour liquid—he tasted flecks of it in his mouth, bile again—floated through his abdomen. Were his eyes closing, or was some brightness gone? Miriam stepped out of his short story. He saw the vacuum she left behind, a blank white silhouette. Everything else was alive, multicolored. Only she was cut out of the page, leaving a blank white silhouette.

What now? The story was dead. Shultish was mildly curious about the ending. But never mind. Some other time. Miriam, her soldier, and the tape had completely broken his Bar-Nun mood. A man has to have a heroine to make a story; he has to love the heroine; and she has to give her creator her undivided attention. But Miriam had betrayed him. She stole herself from him, snapped his link with Bar-Nun. That handclasp broke so many things, unlinked so many things. If she stepped out of the tape, would the tape crumble, like the jigsaw puzzle? The gears ground. The bus was making the steep ascent to the crown of the Carmel. The sea suddenly appeared at Shultish's left—a ring of still blue. No drama was greater than that sudden bluing of the sea. It resembled music after silence, water after thirst. He felt the ascent in his ears. Swallowed. Felt a concomitant rise in his spirits. He had seen his sea again. He wondered for a moment why he felt so good, then realized: I didn't make a fool with myself with her after all, thank God. I retained my illusions. I kept my dignity.

The gravel path to Bar-Nun's house moved like an escalator leading to the door. He stood in the shade of a fir tree and looked down at the Mediterranean. Before him was the entire curve of the bay, from Haifa to Acco. The day was clear. Rosh Hanikra and the Lebanese range to the north were perfectly visible. Strange how the weather determined distance. On a dry, clear day one could almost touch the mountains. Of course the view would be better from Bar-Nun's library, where it was unobstructed on four sides. The fabled view. Inaccessible. A breeze came from the north. Shultish took a deep breath. Scents of clover, honeysuckle, and pine mingled in the air. He felt buoyant again, standing at the top of the world, about to get his tape again. One girl lost, another found. Not too long ago he had stood at this very time on this very spot. Then he was about to get the tape, not yet possessing it but enjoying the sensation of imminent possession. Now he already had it—it existed—it really was in his possession. He only had to reclaim ownership.

Bar-Nun opened the door before Shultish had a chance to ring. Not only did Bar-Nun not embrace him, he did not even shake his hand.

"Ah, Shultish. I've been waiting for you. Here, not a moment's waiting. Here, here is the tape. Safely into the pocket now. Good. Careful with it." Bar-Nun slipped it into Shultish's inside jacket pocket.

"And *how!*" Shultish patted it to see if the tape was still there. "You don't know what miserable days I've had. It affected other things too, the loss of the tape. My relations with people. My own writing."

"Really? Your own writing!" Bar-Nun clapped his hands in

commiseration. "I am so sorry. Had I known I would have called you sooner. But I truly did not want to upset you—"

"It's all right. The main thing is I have it now."

For a moment they stood facing each other. Shultish did not know what to do. He heard the ticking of his watch, slower, quicker, following his heart. Embarrassed, he lowered his eyes. His heart made the watch tick slower, until he could count the waiting seconds between each tick. At other times, when he was with Bar-Nun, the meetings had been prearranged and the subjects of conversation set; most of the time other people were present and there was no time to speak. Now he felt like an intruder, one who had burst into the author's house without an appointment, just for a glimpse of the famous man, and had not the faintest notion of what to say except gape and stammer out a request for an autograph.

Shultish glanced up at the stairway that led to the library and was about to tell Bar-Nun that he had to be going now. But Bar-Nun placed a finger on his lips as though hinting that Shultish should not say good-bye.

"Tell me Shultish, *yedidi,* I want to ask you something. Did you really want the tape? Be frank. Now that you have it, you can tell me the truth."

"Of course," Shultish said. "Why do you ask?"

Bar-Nun moved his finger from his lips and dug it into his cheek. The skin on his hands was like leather, and when his hands moved, wrinkles like lines in a magnetic field went through them. But the rest of him, except for the slow walk, was young. What made Bar-Nun so youthful?

"Because you forgot it. Although I know nothing about psychology, it seems to me that if you want something very badly you don't lose it. You only forget things you really want to put out of mind. Perhaps you wanted the *idea* of my recording it—much as a man goes after an elusive girl—more than the recording itself."

Shultish put his finger on his cheek for a moment, then pressed his hand to his chest. "Permit me to say, *Adon* Bar-Nun, that like you I too am not a student of psychology. But since you mention the psychological standpoint, perhaps I should say that if a person wants something very much and cares for it greatly, his worry over it is so profound that a partial collapse of sensibility occurs. Perhaps, in fact, that is what did happen with the tape.'' Shultish patted his jacket pocket again to reassure himself and said again, ''The main thing is I have it now.''

''Amen,'' Bar-Nun replied, then put his hand to his mouth in a gesture of surprise. ''Amen? Did my ears hear what my lips have uttered? You see how God places reminders on man's lips. I said amen automatically. But there is nothing automatic in man that doesn't have a deeper meaning. That's another thing that I don't know about psychology. The amen served as a reminder to me. Look at the hour. Have you said the afternoon prayers yet?'' Bar-Nun asked quickly.

''I haven't,'' said Shultish. He gingerly put his hand to his head to check that the skullcap was there.

Bar-Nun went to another table and picked up a little prayer-book. ''Here. Use this. It's my own Siddur. And by the time you're finished I'll have come down from the library with a little surprise for you.''

Shultish took the prayerbook. Yes, it was the one Bar-Nun had offered his son-in-law. Leipzig, 1860. Its top and bottom edges were gilded. The print was tiny but sharp. No doubt about it, they made beautiful prayerbooks in the old days. And the thin pages were well thumbed, contrary to reports that Bar-Nun just posed as, was not really, a religious man. Shultish opened to the Afternoon Service, faced Jerusalem, and began to read, not pray. Yes, he recognized the words. How long it had been since he had seen an Afternoon Service! He wanted to skip a page, just like a youngster in shul, but he didn't dare. He had better *daven,* Shultish thought, because Bar-Nun might be peeking down at him from some hole in the ceiling. He looked at the words. They struck familiar chords but gave him no inner music. It's true, Shultish mused, as God is my witness, I'm not religious. And if I'm not, I who am so close to the classic Hebrew words and classic Hebrew thought, how could anyone else be? How could these youngsters in Israel be religious if they didn't know the words, even though they spoke Hebrew? A Hebrew cleansed of Jewish.

Could it be said, Shultish wondered, could a future critic writing about his contributions to Hebrew culture ever say that Hebraism became his Judaism? A nice phrase, a beautiful phrase. But it wouldn't be true. It could be said of the Israelis, but not of him. He had learned Yiddishkeyt at his father's house, sponged it into his soul, could recognize every nuance of Bible and Talmud and Midrash and Siddur in the literature. But like Ben-Gurion, like all the great modern leaders of Israel, he knew but did not observe.

As he held Bar-Nun's Siddur, his eyes scanned and his lips said the words, but his heart was upstairs, wondering what surprise Bar-Nun had prepared for him. An invitation to come up to the library? No. That would have been extended immediately. Perhaps the formal invitation to become Bar-Nun's translator? Or an article Bar-Nun had written on Shultish's stories, Bar-Nun's first critique in decades? Bar-Nun already had the galleys or a carbon of the article he had just sent out to his paper, *Ha-et.* The prayers raced by, blessing over blessing. Why did it have to wait till later? What was it? Something in gratitude for the many years he had devoted to his book on Bar-Nun and had not yet even won a prize for?

Shultish stared at the fingers that held Bar-Nun's personal Siddur. As he held the prayerbook, saying the words that Bar-Nun recited daily, he could be Bar-Nun himself. In Bar-Nun's house. Next to his desk. Writer. Nobel Laureate in Literature. The prayers spun themselves out. At the conclusion of the Silent Devotion, Shultish took three steps backwards, looking over his shoulder to see if Bar-Nun was coming. He raced through the *Alenu* and closed the Siddur. Bar-Nun had not yet come. On Bar-Nun's writing table several pens stood in a glass. The pens that Bar-Nun wrote with, created with. The pens Bar-Nun had subdued. Shultish looked quickly at the stairs again. Perhaps he should run up and ask if Bar-Nun was all right. Perhaps the old man needed help. Six or seven pens in the glass. He wouldn't miss one. The pen the

132

master wrote with. Shultish leaned forward, held one of them. If Shultish would write with Bar-Nun's pen, his writing would improve. The pen, thinking it was held by Bar-Nun's fingers, would write like him. What an item to show his students in New York. Ladies and gentlemen, this is the pen that Bar-Nun himself composed with. Yes, looking down shyly, a gift from him. A little memento. Not *memento mori,* God forbid, but *memento vivere. Memento creato.* He had prayed with Bar-Nun's Siddur, become for a moment Bar-Nun in worship; now the pen. Pen, Siddur, words. How else could he become Bar-Nun?

"Shultish, just a moment. I'm coming down." Bar-Nun said from upstairs.

Pen clicked back in glass.

The surprise, Shultish thought. Bar-Nun walked slowly down.

"Look, Shultish."

Shultish saw the manuscript before he saw it. An article entitled "The Fiction of Ezra Shultish," by Yehiel Bar-Nun. The recognition far outweighed any prize.

"Look, Shultish!"

From behind his back

"Surprise!"

Bar-Nun showed him a photograph, a browning snapshot of Bar-Nun smiling in front of a doorway and standing next to half of a shy young man, sliced lengthwise.

"Remember? Nachmani took the picture."

Shultish held the picture in his hand, at arm's length, focusing on it. It looked like Bar-Nun years ago, but who was the foolish half-chap staring into the lens?

"Who's the half-noodle?"

"Shultish, my dear, don't you recognize yourself? The Midrash states that man's image of himself never changes. Have you forgotten your own image?"

"Me? Is that *me?*"

"Don't you remember? In Vienna? The first time you came to visit me. Nachmani—then he was still Nachmanovitz—was there with his first camera. Surely you remember the old philosopher

133

with his doddering old voice"—here Bar-Nun gave an excellent imitation—"calling us outside for a snapshot. Insisting that even though life was an illusion, man could be photographed?"

"It's extraordinary, *Adon* Bar-Nun. I remember everything about that visit. There was a new book by Bialik on your desk. He had just phoned. I could write down every word we said even now, thirty-two years later, and yet I'd forgotten that incident completely."

Bar-Nun waved a finger. "There's a good reason for it. Listen. It's because Nachmani cut half your head off lengthwise. He sliced the part of your brain that stores the memory. You knew that only half of you would appear in the picture, so you only half remembered. And if something is not whole, it tends to diminish quickly. And so half remembered soon faded into not remembered."

"It's still a historic picture."

"I would have sent it to you, but I didn't have your address."

"Do you think I could borrow it for a while to have a copy made? Today they have excellent methods of copying a photograph. It doesn't even damage the original."

"It's yours, Shultish."

"Mine?"

"Yes. The surprise."

"You're too kind, *Adon* Bar-Nun. First the tape, the use of your Siddur, and now this historic snapshot. Thank you so much."

Bar-Nun looked at his watch. "It's getting late."

"Yes, it is," Shultish quickly agreed.

"Fine. Then let me walk you to the bus stop." Bar-Nun went to his closet and took out a coat. Shultish helped him on with it and then rushed to open the door for him. The evening air, mountain cool, flowed in.

"The air of Haifa," Bar-Nun said. "A present from God. The Almighty did not glorify Haifa in the early days. He only mentioned it once in the Talmud. But to make up for this He has given us now the rare gift of Haifa air, in which is concentrated all the sweetness of North and South, East and West of Israel. . . . Come, let us walk slowly to the bus. It's late, true, but we are not in that much of a rush."

"Would you mind if I asked you a question about a story?"

"For you, anything, Shultish. Just no interpretation. People press me for interpretations until my head aches. Once a man is given a prize, people discover him. What do I mean by this, what do I mean by that? Especially since the Nobel Prize. Perfect strangers. Who have never even read a word I wrote."

"I knew more than thirty years ago you'd get the Nobel Prize. I knew it in your house that day Nachmani took the picture, but I was too timid to say it. I thought it would be too presumptuous for an eighteen-year-old youth."

"Old friends and readers are different. That's why I'll answer any question for you, *yedidi,* but no interpretations, please. Not even for you will I do that."

"God forbid! I wouldn't take your secrets. I just wanted to ask you how you came to write 'The Yemenite Girl.' "

Bar-Nun stopped by a little clearing overlooking the sea. He scanned the horizon. Looking for what? Mermaids?

"That I'll tell you, Shultish. Why not? With pleasure. But don't quote me. Don't go rushing out to write an article on it. For it happened so long ago that the story assumes a life of its own and overwhelms memory. I no longer really know how to separate fiction from memory. And I don't care to. Let the critics, the historians do that. Let the late Langweil write monographs for the angels. They too, poor things, need to be put to sleep. . . . See how many jobs I've created? In heaven and on earth. Now to your question. If I remember correctly, it happened when I lived in Rishon and would go bathing to the sea. I saw there a pretty Yemenite girl who— No . . . no . . . I'm sorry. You see what I mean? That's from the story. . . . Wait a minute." Bar-Nun closed his eyes and pressed his fist into the bridge of his nose. "Aha! Now I remember. . . . She was the maid of Shpieglshtein, the artist. You know, the one who made the famous portrait of Herzl standing in Rishon with the first colonists. I would see her there, and then one morning, on her day off, I bumped into her by the dunes."

"And her father wasn't—?" Shultish asked.

"Not that I recall."

"But that situation is so similar to—"

"To what?"

"Did Yarkoni tell you anything?" Shultish asked.

"Far vos hot ir zakh tsugetshepet letstens tsu Yarkoni," Bar-Nun said in Yiddish, asking why Shultish was so interested in Yarkoni lately. It was the first time in Shultish's memory that Bar-Nun had expressed himself in juicy, homey Yiddish, a language Shultish had been longing to hear him speak.

"Well, I thought he told you—because I'm working on a similar story."

"Don't worry." Bar-Nun smiled, putting his arm around Shultish's shoulders. "Do you see the Mediterranean out there? It's just sea water. Most people can't tell one sea from another. After all, salt water is salt water. But there *is* a difference. Color, smell, essence. Each sea is different; each has a character of its own. Same thing with stories. God gave man seven seas, but only two or three stories. Then it's man's challenge to make those stories say thousands of different things. So even if it *is* the same story, try another variation. That's the challenge, the secret of writing. You like music, Shultish."

"Well, I—"

"So I'll accommodate you with an analogy from music, which as you well know I know nothing about and like even less. God gave eight notes to man, and look how many different noises he can make with them. There's no end to the variations. . . ." Bar-Nun took Shultish's arm and continued his stroll. *"Yedidi,* do you want to hear a story?"

"What a question! I'm always ready to hear a story from you."

Bar-Nun stopped to take a breath. Shultish heard the wind rushing into Bar-Nun's lungs. Bar-Nun breathing. The night air. Shultish aware of crickets and trees. Up there the moon was split into fragments by the moving branches.

"This is one, Ezra—"

A bell sans sound sprayed colors in Shultish's head. He replayed the conversation, found he had heard correctly. He called me

Ezra. Not Shultish. For the first time. He always refers to other people by their family names. Gutman, Yarkoni, Gershoni, Malkin, Grumkin, Lumkin. I'm really one of the family now: Ezra.

"—that I haven't published yet. It links up with the past and looks to the future. Once—"

"Yehiel! Yehiel!"

Both men turned. A woman approached quickly.

"Ah, my dear! Rivka Orman!" Bar-Nun stretched out both his hands, then took her right hand and kissed it. "When did you get back? How is your husband? Is he well?"

"Yesterday. We stopped off at Venice, too. He's fine," she said breathlessly. "We saw your son." She put her hands on her chest, catching her breath.

"Easy. Easy." Bar-Nun touched her shoulder. "No rush. The Sabbath doesn't come in for another forty-eight hours."

"Avraham sends regards."

"Mrs. Orman is a very special person," Bar-Nun said, his eyes sparkling, greening like a tiger's in the night. He took her hand again, addressing Shultish but looking at the woman. "This is Ezra Shultish, a Hebrew writer and teacher from America. I don't mention his distinguished book about me first, so that God forbid I won't be accused of immodesty."

Shultish shook hands with the woman.

"Why does Yehiel Bar-Nun say that I'm a special person?" Mrs. Orman smiled, looking to Bar-Nun—a quick glance at Shultish—as though to continue a line that had been rehearsed many times.

"Because she named two of her children after characters in my first novella," Bar-Nun told Shultish, and smiled at Mrs. Orman. Then Bar-Nun stepped closer, took hold of Shultish's jacket—that close stance in speaking that East Europeans used, which Westerners found disturbing, too intimate for comfort. "The first Hebrew children in Israel with names like that: Alim and Geza."

Shultish opened his mouth.

"I know what you'll say." Mrs. Orman held up her hand. "They're both popular names. *Now*. But thirty years ago? We were the first."

"Look in the registration archives," Bar-Nun said.

"The power of a writer," Mrs. Orman said, then laughed to take the edge off the solemnity.

Her name was Orman. Outwardly an Ashkenazi name. Yet she did not look like a European. Her Hebrew accent was too good for her to stem from Poland or Russia. On the other hand, she did not look Oriental either. Shultish watched Mrs. Orman conversing with Bar-Nun; she told him about things bought in Europe. He asked prices. There was a practiced rhythm and humor in their talking, as if they had known each other for years. She was in her fifties, Shultish was certain, yet she was still beautiful. The Yemenite girl?

Trivia, trivia, Shultish told himself. Instead of talking to me about literature, he's talking about shopping and prices. You're a robber, he told the woman. Precious moments wasted. Shultish wished he were a ventriloquist and could call the woman away, throw his voice to the balcony across the way and whisper, "Mrs. Orman, Mrs. Orman." By force of will, Shultish held back the bus. He slowed it up, put more lights on the route, made red lights longer. It backed up traffic in town, but Shultish did not care. At one red light he made the driver jump out to a kiosk—he had seen them do it on buses he rode—and buy a pack of cigarettes, missing a green light and having to wait through an extra red. But still Bar-Nun and Mrs. Orman kept talking. Shultish did not know how much longer ʰe would be able to continue holding back the bus. It was no easy task. Joshua had held back the sun, stopped time. He too had held the sun in hand, once, long ago, for a precious moment. Keeping back the bus was no trifle, either. It was like holding one's breath for three minutes. Unless he purposely missed one bus and nonchalantly told Bar-Nun and the woman that he'd take the next one. But then what would he do if Bar-Nun said, "Ah, here's your bus, Shultish"? Missing it then would be a discourtesy and perhaps peeve the old man, who liked to begin and end visits at his will.

"Ah, I hear your bus, Shultish. It will be here in a minute."

"The story," Shultish protested. He touched his pocket, felt the bulge of the tape.

"Can't now," Bar-Nun protested. "Next time. There is no end

to storytelling. No end to the making of books. Here's your bus. Good night."

"Good night. Good night, Mrs. Orman."

Shultish walked to the bus stop, hearing

"Rivka, remember what I once told you about politics in my work?"

but there was no turning back now. The bus pulled in to the stop. The door opened. Shultish fumbled for change.

"But the critics," Mrs. Orman said.

One step up, looking back.

"All the critics are wrong. And *langweilig* to boot. Like musicians they're blind to the reality around them."

Bar-Nun waved good-bye.

As Shultish sat in the bus, the biblical verse, "No end to the making of books," rang, repeated in his mind. He looked out the window and could barely make out a dark figure, a black silhouette, not blank or white as Miriam's had been, walking through the night cricket sounds. That Mrs. Orman, with her sons out of a Bar-Nun novella, came along at the wrong moment. She had deprived him of a Bar-Nun story—but gained him a book. Why had Bar-Nun told him about the children named after his characters? Shultish touched his pocket. Tape still there. Because he wanted to hint that Mrs. Orman was the Yemenite girl but could not because she was standing there. Shultish tried to recall her features and mold her into the story. But Miriam intruded, montaged into Mrs. Orman and distorted her. In one thought the models for Bar-Nun's version and his version of "The Yemenite Girl" blended. Past and future. That's what Bar-Nun meant. He wanted to tell me about the original Yemenite girl, and then unwittingly introduced me to her. Now Shultish didn't know whom to blame and whom to thank. Once again someone had intruded on his privacy with Bar-Nun, but on the other hand this time it had been a fortunate meeting. Now he had the real-life model for his favorite story, in addition to a tape of it as read by the author himself. He tapped his pocket again, slipped his hand in and held the tape. Still there. And then the surprise, a newly discovered picture of himself—well, really half of himself—with the master. Although Shultish had just discovered it, actually he had been in that picture for more than three decades. Side by side with Bar-Nun. And now he had so many things of Bar-Nun's, including his friendship—elevated to a first-name basis—the use of Bar-Nun's Siddur, and a model for a short story. What more could he want before becoming the man himself? Shultish's head whirled. Wait, he thought. There was something else. Politics. Bar-Nun had spoken to Mrs. Orman but actually addressed Shultish. "No end to the making of books." Directed at Shultish. As in a delirium "The Yemenite Girl" tumbled in his mind. Shultish had to extirpate history and tradition from it now and seek politics. Whom did the Yemenite girl stand for? And the narrator? Who was he? Wait. Perhaps Bar-Nun was being ironical again. But if not, Shultish had had a private revelation, worth far more than an ephemeral peek at Israel from Bar-Nun's library. A revelation and a command for a new book: *Bar-Nun and the State Order: A Study in Literature and Politics,* by Ezra Shultish. Perhaps in another *gilgul* he'd be reborn Bar-Nun himself. But then who would be Shultish? Gutman, he decided. It would serve him right.

What went through my mind then? What did not go through my mind then? I pictured many things. I pictured myself at my writing desk at the slab of flat stone on the jetty, composing various alternatives that were washed away by the sea, as a sponge washes chalk from slate.

The evening bus ride was soothing, surrounded by the sea. At an intersection Shultish saw two men lighting cigarettes at the same time. Both had lighters with overlarge flames. He had a sudden idea and felt a new spirit surging into him. He couldn't hold it in his hands, yet he could touch it. Like the Yemenite girl, like Miriam. He loved its taste, the new spirit. Sweet and winy, it went to his head like muscatel. The birth of a brilliant idea and its businesslike execution. At home he works on it. First, the invitations to all of Israel's men of letters to join a torchlight parade from the Carmel to its crown, to the old man's house. A birthday surprise for the classic writer. No one left out. Major and minor figures. Even prima donnas do not demur. In Haifa everyone helps Shultish for the big event. Even Gutman's boss, the old archivist Naamani himself, puts his office at Shultish's disposal. Then a letter, in many carbons—there is only so much secretarial help—to all the newspapers: Alert your reporters! Top secret. What a gift for the old man by all the Hebrew culture leaders of Israel and the Diaspora. A tribute by young and old. Later, Shultish remembered the headlines, second page in most papers, but first page in *Ha-et*. Naturally, the paper that published Bar-Nun stories would frontpage the event. At first the flash bulbs disturbed Shultish, but when he saw his picture with that of Bar-Nun on *Ha-et's* front page, with torches in the background, and a paragraph on his link to, and his work about, Bar-Nun, he soared to another world. No doubt sales of his book would rise. Perhaps it would even be recommended for one of Israel's literary prizes.

The torches on that moonlit night lit up the sky. Through the darkness came the procession, each man with his torch. Gutman's boss had even been helpful in other ways, despite the fact that he was boiling with envy at Gutman's Fichman Prize. One hand washed the other, as the Yiddish saying had it. Naamani had dealt out favors; now was the time to cash in. With the police chief, no traffic. With the chief electrician, no traffic lights. Shultish wondered what it would cost him, those favors. Small chance. What favors had he to offer? If Shultish had been in a helicopter he might have been able to see the serpentine procession. A living library of writers. Each man representing hundreds of books, stories, and critiques. "Literature on the March," one headline called it. A birthday gift by a grateful nation. When the procession stopped, Bar-Nun emerged to see why lights had suddenly flooded his secluded spot. Poor man, he must have thought it was a fire. Why had night suddenly turned into day?

No one spoke when Bar-Nun appeared except Potemkowitz, Habimah's oldest actor, a genius in his eighties, with his rolling r's and Russian accent, one of the founding fathers of the Hebrew National Theater in Moscow. In the silence he cleared his throat in preparation for the reading from Bar-Nun's works. Another surprise for the old man.

By now neighbors have gathered on the balconies to watch the unannounced parade. A circle of lights has formed in Bar-Nun's yard. He opens the door. For the first time in his life he does not know what to say. Potemkowitz raises his left hand in a majestic sweep, lifts his chin, and brings the book into reading position with his right. A signal for silence. Potemkowitz begins to read. Shultish stands in the shadow of the portable spotlight. He sees the flickering of the hundreds of torchlights on all the faces. The old actor reads from one of Bar-Nun's novels. As in a synagogue, there is no applause after the reading. Through the shifting lights Shultish moves forward to Bar-Nun and presents him with a scroll wishing him health and long years. It is signed by all the writers of the People of Israel. A light flashes. It annoys Shultish, but then he realizes what it was. Photographed. All of him, he hopes. Not half. Shultish examines Bar-Nun's face. Are those tears in Bar-Nun's eyes, or is it a reaction to the sudden bright light?

Bar-Nun raises his hands.

"I have written many words on paper, few on air. The words I've written on paper are for you, my teachers and masters, for I have learned from all of you. Those here, those not here. May the God of Israel bless you, the writers of Israel, for coming up to the crown of the Carmel which overlooks the entire Land of Israel."

And Bar-Nun throws Shultish a special look of intimacy and recognition, singling him out among all the individualists who have consented to leave their own spotlights to become part of the mass.

The light spins. Some torches waver, tumble upside down. Shultish stops short. Forward in his seat. Bar-Nun sails past. The bus has braked to avoid a bicycle. The driver swiftly sticks his head out the window.

"You ass!"

Shultish blinked, looked for the torchlight. Saw streetlights instead. Blinked again, then again. The torchlight he wanted to see glowed for a moment on a distant screen, then turned to darkness. Hand to pocket, touching, seizing, saving what was real, he clutched the tape in his fist, locked as though in a dead man's fingers.

When I thought of the sea, I thought of life. And yet thinking of the sea reminded me of futility; for eternity the waves kept rushing toward the shore, but all in vain; the five or six meters they gained in the morning they lost that afternoon. Yet the waves and wavelets maintained their stubborn attempt to storm the shore.

Shultish lay in bed unable to sleep. Some epitaph. Some message to eternity. Hebraism became his Judaism. Waves from the sea thronged forward, lapping laving lulling him almost to sleep, but missing, like water slipping through fingers. The prayerbook suddenly clutched at his hand, the one held by, owned by, Bar-Nun. Then, in a flash of its gilt-edged pages, it was gone. Shultish didn't need it: he knew the words by heart, even though he hadn't said them in decades. He knew the meaning, knew the sources. He shook his head. His New York students would know a story by an Israeli writer, but the Siddur was closed to them. To give them a reference from a prayer, a bit of folklore, a phrase from the Talmud, a hint from ritual, was to knock your head against a wall. To them the words of the Silent Devotion or the Grace After Meals were isolated, dictionary-heavy, unlinked to the past. How would these youngsters be able to teach others, even with their pathetic degrees from the Hebrew Teachers Academy? Well, they could use the footnotes that had to be included even in Israeli editions of Bar-Nun's works for schoolchildren. The sabras, teachers and students, had to work with a pony. Shultish remembered his shock when he first saw footnotes for words like mezuza, Siddur, and dozens of other terms that a European Jew or a Talmud Torah pupil in America took for granted: "Tefillin: a kind of black box, with leather straps attached, containing passages from the Torah, worn on weekdays by male Orthodox Jews over thirteen during morning prayers."

The footnotes had an even greater impact when he mulled them over in his mind. My Lord, this is an ominous symbol. I should write about it. Tefillin and Siddur have to be footnoted for Jews in Israel. A wave of chills rippled down his back. Bad business. In Israel, Hebrew had become divorced from Jewish. "Hebrew and Jewish: Language and Cultural Consciousness in Israel" by Ezra Shultish.

His generation of nonreligious Diaspora-born Hebrew teachers who had loved Zion but were lukewarm to ritual had raised a generation of Hebrew-loving Israeli Jews who held the Diaspora in contempt. Thank God he'd been in New York, so he couldn't be blamed for *that*. But the Gutmans had taught their subject so well that they had become the perfect teachers. Their students knew their subjects so well that they had no further use for them. Bialik and European-Jewish culture, the shtetl, tefillin, mezuza—all that was foreign and ludicrous to them. But in New York, Hebraism wasn't so ludicrous, because there one could claim it as a kind of salvation. A substitute for Yiddishkeyt, a substitute for Israel. No wonder Shimshovitz loved Hebrew so much. In New York one could afford the luxury of a secular Hebraism. But Israel, Shultish realized, Israel could not. In Israel, Hebrew culture without the values and knowledge of Yiddishkeyt smacked of . . . Shultish turned in his bed. Somewhere a cuckoo clanged. A pine tree lit up in his mind; a cuckoo in a pine tree would not go away. A cuckoo calling in a tinseled pine. If the old abandoned the ways, if atheism wormed its way into Israel, what hope was there for the young? A pain rose, flashed and abated in his abdomen. A cool breeze came into the room. He filled his lungs, sighed. Yes, it smacked of Hellenism. Something foreign. An alien culture. Rootless.

And anyway, the future critic writing about his contributions (oh, modest contributions, he knew; only a parenthesis, a footnote in some very slim and perhaps never-to-be-published *History of Hebrew in America*)—that critic would be dead wrong if he said of Shultish: Hebraism was his Judaism. Shultish shook his head in the dark. The cuckoo stopped. Why, he even—secret message, private lust—thought, dreamed in English; he didn't even have enough determination, as some colleagues did, to insist that

Hebrew be spoken in the home. To whom? The children he'd never had?

Shultish sat up in bed, alone in the darkness, "I am in Israel," he said. Alone, echoed his mind, "I am in Israel," he incanted. Alone, came the echo. "I am in Israel," he repeated, to drive away the loneliness, the gloom, that emptiness which elusive fingers, the fingers that his fingers didn't have, could not capture or subdue.

THREE

Three days passed. Three days of calm, of sunshine, of afternoon naps. Three days of riding the distant blue waves. Shultish first heard the report on the ten o'clock evening news. He had tuned in at one minute after ten · The familiar announcer's voice was saying: "... in the Haifa Hospital this evening of a heart attack. The funeral will be tomorrow at two P.M. in Jerusalem. The President of Israel has declared tomorrow a national day of mourning . . ."

"Shultish? Gutman. Have you heard?"

"Yes and no. I tuned in late, just as they were saying 'in the Haifa Hospital . . . of a heart attack.' I didn't actually hear who, but my heart tells me. The national day of mourning proclaimed by the President tells me. And I had plans of organizing a torchlight procession to his house. In honor of his birthday. Assembling all the writers of Israel. A surprise for—"

"In the next world, Shultish. Now they'll all meet tomorrow in Jerusalem."

"Oh, God. God, God, God!"

"What is it, Shultish? Are you crying?"

"I just realized. Oh, God. Gutman!"

"I know how you feel. Believe me, I feel the same way."

"It's something else. I have to talk to you."

"Now?"

"Don't sound so peeved. It's only five minutes after ten. You're not in your pajamas, are you?"

"Of course not. It's not that. It's just that—is it something serious?"

"I'll be over right away."

As Shultish knocked, he recalled that long ago—when he was young—Miriam would open the door to welcome him. But now he heard heavier footfalls. Not Miriam's. Miriam would not greet him at night, because she worked only by day. And since it was night, there was no Miriam. Miriam was holding hands somewhere with her boy friend, embracing him as she had embraced the grocery bags that Shultish had seized when, for a moment, he had embraced Miriam too. There was no Miriam. He had not come to see Miriam now.

"*Shalom,* Shultish. Come in. Let's sit in the kitchen and have some tea, eh? You don't mind, do you? Sarah is already in bed."

"Fine. Perfect," he said, looking around to see if Miriam would flit by from the kitchen, bringing tea. "We can talk in the kitchen."

Gutman put water on to boil. They sat and stared at each other and then lowered their eyes. Gutman made tea, found some dry biscuits. Shultish sipped slowly. He had no appetite for cookies. The hot liquid burned his tongue, barely pushed down the iron ball in his chest. Gutman stirred the sugar in his glass. The glass settled poorly on the saucer. Gutman's hand shook. The porcelain noise clattered in the little room.

I killed him, Shultish said, looking down into the glass, seeing Bar-Nun's face there, not his own. I killed the greatest writer in the world.

"This evening. At six. How a heart attack can finish a man," Gutman said, not looking at Shultish.

Shultish blew at his tea. He moved closer to the table. His

heartbeat knocked against the wood. The kettle was still boiling, sending out a shaft of steam. The lid tapped erratically on the rim. At first its unrhythm bothered Shultish, then it pleased him. He tried to anticipate the beat of the lid dance. He picked up his teaspoon and watched his image on the convex side of the stainless steel.

"No need talking, Shultish. I understand," Gutman said.

No you don't, Shultish said. I'm selfish. I made him record for me. A sick man. Tired. Out of breath. I put a strain on him, Gutman. I heard the way he breathed. I should have known. He breathed heavily. Like sighs. Just to satisfy myself and have that recording, I made him exert himself.

You're mad, Gutman said. A fifteen-minute recording? You're going out of your mind. That's what happens when a man reads only one author and hasn't got a wife at home to keep him stable.

"She's coming home. She's coming home."

"Who?" Gutman asked.

"Shoshana. Soon."

Gutman shut off the gas. "How are you going, Shultish? Car or train?"

"Train. You know I don't have a car. And you?"

"I'm going with the archives people."

"Is there—"

"No. I'm sorry, the car is full. There'll be plenty of people on the train, though. You'll have company."

"Two weeks ago he recorded for me," Shultish said. "And I just saw him three days ago."

"Many things can happen even in a day."

Shultish, nodding, rose. Gutman pressed his hand with both hands, consoling him. He walked Shultish to the door. "Careful crossing the streets, *yedidi.*"

Shultish took an early morning train. Sleepy, exhausted from the night's dream, he listened to the talk of Bar-Nun around him but said nothing. Only in Israel, Shultish thought, would the authorities add trains in honor of a writer. Instead of the six and ten o'clock trains to Jerusalem, the Israel Railways was running a train every half hour.

The full force of Bar-Nun's passing had not struck him till that morning. Dreams that Bar-Nun was alive alternated with sudden waking to reality. He felt his strength ebbing. A hole in his heart, a hole revolving and enlarging. Like hunger pangs. No longer here. No longer here, came the clatter of the wheels. Shultish did not want to talk. He closed his eyes and leaned his head against the head rest, surrounded by conversations about Bar-Nun. If the other riders thought he was sleeping they would not bother him. He would not have to relate how he felt now, and how he felt the moment he had heard the news; he would not have to tell them where and when he had first heard. By pretending to sleep he could absorb gossip without contributing any of his own. And perhaps someone would recognize him from the picture on the jacket of his Bar-Nun book. He'd be pointed out, and whispers of praise, not meant for his ears, would come to him.

Behind him someone said: "They wanted to bury him on Mount Herzl with—"

"Mount Herzl? A writer?"

"—the other great men of Israel. Writers, by the way, are not excluded from that category."

"Mount Herzl is only for politicians. Members of government."

"Really? What about Jabotinsky? What government did he serve in? What about Herzl himself?"

Bickering, petty bickering, Shultish thought. All they know is how to fill up space with hot air, contentious words.

"And they *would* have buried him on Mount Herzl if not for the note."

Shultish fought hard not to open his eyes.

"A note? What kind of note?" someone asked. Through closed eyes Shultish saw the man clearly. Thin, fifty-five. Smooth-shaven. A hanger-on, tolerated on the periphery of literary circles. One who in a photograph of writers would be in the last row, near the edge of the snapshot, smiling, craning his neck to get in.

"Who found the note?"

"His son. The Ambassador from Switzerland. He flew in late last night. A special flight. Went to his desk at home and found a note saying that he wished to be buried on the Mount of Olives, above Jerusalem. Bar-Nun buried all his characters there, so why not himself?"

"And I have another story," someone else said. Shultish felt the people near him turning around. "A writer is valuable property when he's alive. Dead he becomes priceless. Speaking of dead, look at this one. Sleeping. He'll sleep through the funeral, too. You want to hear something? Listen to this."

Shultish could not bear it any longer. His lids were tearing open. He opened his eyes an eighth of an inch, parting the curtains to darkness, seeing without being seen.

"Adoni? Adoni, are you asleep?"

Shultish, maintaining even breathing, did not reply.

"Imagine someone sleeping on his way to a funeral."

"He's either asleep or dead. People pretending sleep have a live expression on their face. He looks absolutely blank. The man is obviously dead."

"Does anybody know who he is?"

Shultish heard the men shrugging. He felt a weight in his chest sinking, then pulling the rest of him along with it, as though it sought to turn him upside down, inside out. The soul in him became a little blue knot, receding.

"Nobody knows who he is."

In the distance a door slammed.

"That's Ezra Shultish," a man whispered. "A hanger-on of Bar-Nun's. A teacher from America. He writes, too. He's had his hopes of being his translator."

"Never heard of him."

"Yes, that's Shultish. He's here for a year."

Shultish floated back. The knot in him, from blue to gray to white, rising like a star. Recognized. Saved. Was it Yarkoni?

"Enough of him," someone said. "Don't you want to hear what I have to say?"

Shultish sensed the men turning away from him. "Let's hear it."

"All right. As soon as the Haifa City Hall heard of Bar-Nun's death, may he rest in peace, they decided that they wanted to keep him. The mayor, the Culture Council, the Haifa Tourist Bureau, they all felt that keeping Bar-Nun here, burying him here, building a monument to him here would be good for the city. Of course no one actually said this in so many words, God forbid. They all spoke a coded language, a Kabbala all their own. When the director of tourism said Bar-Nun should be buried on top of Mount Carmel which he had loved so much, you didn't need a biblical commentator like Rashi to tell you he meant that the monument would be a dandy tourist site. When the head of the Culture Council seconded the motion, saying his grave would overlook the sea he loved so well, it meant he had his eyes on the Bar-Nun archives. When the mayor said that Bar-Nun would have wanted to be buried in the beloved city he spent half a century in, it meant he hoped the Bar-Nun museum and study center would be housed in Haifa, supported by state funds. Everyone wants something for himself, but thank goodness the dead man's will prevailed."

"Isn't that from one of Bar-Nun's stories?" someone said softly. Shultish wondered who; perhaps he himself. Who else would know the Bar-Nun material so well? Said in a doze prompted by keeping his eyes closed so long. Faking sleep so well that he finally became tired and fell asleep.

When he awoke he was in Jerusalem.

The black felt fedora Shultish wore was a clamp on his head. As he followed the procession, the heat pressed the hat on his skull; the inner band, hot and wet, grew tighter. Warm air rose, wavered, like that above a radiator on a winter evening. The street was dead—shutters on the windows closed, corrugated iron gratings drawn like window shades. Slowly down Jaffa Road went the procession, past the corner of Ben-Yehuda, past the post office, the city hall, to the open square where once the concrete wall divided Old Jerusalem from New. Shultish wished he had boarded one of the limousines of the procession. He would not last to the Mount of Olives. The sun twisted the clamp tighter on his skull. His head felt deep red. Dry outside, wet within. A roseate film covered his eyes. Sunstroke. Retribution. For killing the old man. For holding his life in his hands, and taking it. And now Shultish, too, dead. Buried next to Bar-Nun. Jerusalem in mourning. The entire crowd honoring Shultish. All of Israel in motion to Jerusalem. Shultish blinked, saw his feet moving. Then he was alive after all. He did not want to die, not even for the honor of being buried beside Bar-Nun. He had come close enough to death that morning, when his soul became a knot of darkening blue and was about to leave him when no one knew who he was. That was dying. Not being known. Dying was someone asking, Who is he? and no one, absolutely no one, knowing. Living, breathing in a vacuum. Unrecognized. Unknown.

People came in and out of the procession. Those who were tired dropped out; others, following the traditional mitzvah of paying one's respects to the dead, joined for a few steps and then retreated. No. He was not going to do that. He was an old friend, an intimate, almost kin. He had known him so many years. On two continents. He has used his Siddur, held his pen, possessed his voice. The old man had embraced him; once, only once, he had even called him "Ezra." When had all this happened? Years ago. Perhaps never. Because it could not be repeated. It wasn't recorded. It was not printed or pictured.

He had risen at five, traveled by bus down from Carmel to lower Haifa and had come by train to Jerusalem. So he was not going to leave the procession now. Shultish lifted his hat for a moment; a little cyclone of air cooled his forehead. The Old City walls came into view, beige in the sunlight. Then he saw buses. Blinked, thinking it was a mirage. Not one bus, but half a dozen. No mirage, miracle. At the square a line of buses. The procession halted. People were silently bidden to board. Seated in the bus, Shultish forgot the heat. He looked out the window. The city walls came closer, closer, until they embraced the bus. Through Jaffa Gate, now in the Old City, Israel's eternal heart.

Shultish felt a hand on his back. Turning, he saw a short stocky man with gold-rimmed glasses staring at him.

"Excuse me, you are Ezra Shultish." The man smiled; small, clever eyes; a gold-capped tooth.

The affirmative declaration pleased Shultish. "Yes?" he questioned in reply.

"Someone at the back of the bus pointed you out."

"And you are—?" Shultish gave the man his hand.

"My name is Moshe Lichtenstein."

Shultish's eyes lit up. "Ah! The Bar-Nun collector. Just recently I heard you on the radio. Please, sit down." Shultish looked at his watch. "Do you think we'll have time now? There's really so much to talk about. . . . What sort of transportation do you have?"

"None . . . I'm going by train."

"Excellent. We'll go back together."

"But you go to Haifa," Lichtenstein said. "I live in Tel Aviv."

"Hmm . . ." Shultish snapped his fingers. "But we can ride halfway together. To Ramle. Then you get off and board the Tel Aviv train."

"Wonderful."

"You see," Shultish said, elated, "it takes a foreigner to teach an Israeli how to ride an Israeli train."

"*Adon* Shultish," Lichtenstein reprimanded, "you are a Jew, not a foreigner. It is not the foreigner but the Jew in you that knows how to ride an Israeli train."

"Well spoken. A line worthy of Bar-Nun himself."

Lichtenstein smiled. "I suppose when a man has contact with an author for so long, he cannot help being influenced by him. Contact with a man teaches you much, don't you think so?"

"True, one is always learning. For instance, just the last time I saw him, only four days ago, he told me how he came to write 'The Yemenite Girl,' " and Shultish repeated the story that the writer had told him.

"That's very interesting. I heard another version. From his publisher. It seems that it wasn't a Yemenite girl at all, but a girl who had a Yemenite father and a Rumanian mother. And the romance wasn't as tragic as the story would have us believe."

"Is that so? Then would he have known her later too? She couldn't be his neighbor, could she?"

"Well, I don't really like to get into the details of gossip. That would be encroaching on his privacy. And it's outside of my interest. . . . Ah, we're almost there. I'll find you later, on the train." Lichtenstein, despite the bumpy ride, gave a little European bow. "Pleasant meeting you," he said formally.

The bus stopped. Are we at the Mount of Olives already? Then he recognized the Wall, remembered the old custom of a funeral procession stopping at all holy sites along the way. Bar-Nun was now having his last look at the Western Wall of the Ancient Temple. The buses moved again, out the gate of the walled city into the road. A fine dust rose and settled in the bus. To Shultish's right was a deep valley studded by little square white houses that blended into the terrain. The outskirts of Jerusalem might have looked like this during Temple times. Farther up the slope more white squares—the restored graves of the Mount of Olives, which had been desecrated and paved over by the Jordanians. In the distance, on the Jericho road, gleamed the village of El Azariya, and beneath were the tourist sites: the conical Absalom's Tomb, and the onion-domed Russian church like something out of a Kremlin scene. Then Bar-Nun appeared, a bizarre photo-sculpture on one of the onions; Bar-Nun's face as he looked on the thirty-year-old photograph. Then half of Shultish appeared, dangling in midair.

Cut off by an invisible line. Try as he would, Shultish could not create the rest of himself. Only a ghostlike snowstorm image. Why had Bar-Nun given him that picture the very last time they were together? Before he even had time to analyze it, the answer flashed: Bar-Nun had given him that half-picture as a symbolic gesture. For the old man did nothing, either in life or print, without an allusion. A hint to Shultish that with his wife away he was only half a person, as the Kabbala stated. When Shoshana returned he would be whole again. Resurrected. Given new life. That was Bar-Nun's last message to him. Renewed, especially since Miriam was gone and the master himself, God rest his soul, gone too. Now his wife, his other half, would return and he would be whole again. A whole writer. A whole man.

But it was too bad that he could not recall what he looked like thirty years ago. And now it was too late to appear in another photograph with the old man. One thing he lacked: a full picture of himself with Bar-Nun. If Shultish could only have had his full face in that old picture. Lichtenstein! Lichtenstein had found Bar-Nun through a photograph by the famous Haifa photographer, Weitzmann. Lichtenstein would introduce him to Weitzmann, and Weitzmann might be able to undo the damage. Perhaps a montage of Shultish and Bar-Nun, to give the impression that they had been photographed together.

He would call Bar-Nun and ask him for one final favor. To pose with him for a photograph. Shultish shook his head: What am I doing? Has the heat driven me mad? Bar-Nun was dead. He would never see him again. Shultish was crying; his eyes were dry. No more calls from Bar-Nun. No more calls to him. Too late to ask to see Bar-Nun's library. Another thing denied to him. Of course, eventually he would see it. They'd turn the house into a museum and he'd go up to the library and a guard would explain what was here and why it was here and when it was acquired. He would speak in a mechanical voice as though a record were in him. He'd look very officious and tell people—even Shultish!—not to touch anything, but Shultish, even though he had never been there, would know every inch of the place and would be able to tell the guard a thing or two. Seeing the library in the company of a guard would not be the same. He had missed a grand opportunity. He shouldn't have been so shy. He should have had more *chutzpa*. How do others get what they want? They don't keep their mouths shut. Too late. Now Bar-Nun was between home and grave, followed by all those who loved him, by all those who were jealous of him, by all those who did not know what to make of him.

At the graveside were the family, members of the government, all the men of letters, young and old. Shultish could have led the parade, but now he was merely following it.

He nodded to his friends, to his acquaintances. All were transformed. With hats on—hats they wore only for weddings and funerals and perhaps Yom Kippur attendance—all looked like the

Jews they would have looked like had they remained in the Old World, and had the Old World remained what it was. Among the mourners Shultish noted an old man with a wizened face. Bareheaded. Naturally, Shultish thought, Gershoni wouldn't even wear a skullcap. That goy. Maybe next he'll take out a little cross or a miniature Christmas tree, that doddering old man, and stroke it for all to see. Or, to please his wife, and to get even with Bar-Nun for winning the Nobel Prize, the prize he felt belonged to him, he'd make a sign of the cross over the coffin. Why Gershoni was here Shultish had not the faintest notion, except perhaps to proclaim his existence. To prove that the short story he had managed to get published was really not posthumous. And the bare head, of course, was to call attention to himself.

Old Gershoni still had strength enough to look smug, as if he'd outwitted the Angel of Death and looked at anyone who died as being a weak-willed and weakly constituted creature. No sense greeting him. Not to be remembered was the same as being snubbed. He'd have to repeat his name a dozen times and finally be called Mr. Esrog again. He looked at Gershoni's hand. Moving in his pocket. Could not believe his eyes. Turned away, stared again. It was true. Old Gershoni, it seemed, was scratching himself. What exactly he was doing, Shultish could not tell. Was it an itch in the crotch, or was Gershoni affirming life in the midst of death? His youth, his strength, over Bar-Nun's impotence? The scene was so absurd that Shultish almost burst out laughing. The old man was showing his contempt to the very last for the man whose writings he despised, for the man who got the Nobel Prize instead of him. I'm young, strong, alive, Gershoni was trying to say, working up life, showing signs of survival.

Gershoni, Baptist and onanist, what next?

Next to Gershoni stood Lumkin, a pained expression on his face, as though he were attempting to decide who'd get the next literary prize. Shultish moved up a bit so Lumkin would see him, remember him. Perhaps there would be a Bar-Nun Memorial Prize, granted yearly for work done on Bar-Nun. But Shultish could not propose it, for then he would have to exclude himself.

159

He found himself next to Gershoni. Gershoni had finished what he had been doing and his hands were now folded over his chest. So he had stopped this public self-abuse, the ninety-nine-year-old man. Gershoni gave Shultish that faraway look—from the eighteenth century it seemed—head back, mouth slightly open, the false teeth not quite in place, glance through thick glasses. "Mr. Esrog." Gershoni smiled faintly. "I remember you. Yes, I do. The man with the talking machine. It's Mr. Esrog from Haifa," Gershoni said to his wife, who wasn't there. Shultish nodded, restrained himself from looking down at Gershoni's pants. No doubt he wore trousers as old as himself. With buttons, no zipper.

Shultish nodded, bowed, muttered quickly in English, "You're a dirty old man."

The spade worked the earth, metal scraping stone. Back to basics. A raven cawed and flapped long black wings, now larger than an hour ago or an hour hence. Spade dulled thoughts of books, that spade striking earth and stone, that black wingspread of a cawing black raven over the silence. Perhaps it was a trick of optics, but it loomed large against the sky, like a low-flying plane. Shultish heard weeping. He wanted to see the casket being lowered, did not want to see the casket being lowered, and could not get close. The weeping spread. Like a wave? A circle? A stone in water? It touched him. Shultish felt the stares of the family. Guilty, they whispered. I killed him, he said. Mrs. Orman stood next to Bar-Nun's son. She looked coldly at Shultish. I killed him, he said. Gutman shook his head. So many days separated the reading from the heart attack. Not guilty, he whispered. The tears inside him stirred his dry eyes. He loved the old man. Bar-Nun was like a father to him: severe, friendly, paternal. The tears, a wave about to burst. He loved the old man. Flesh of his flesh, in friendship, spirit, thought. The tears blurring his vision. They shared the same words, ideas, literary allusions. The tears; we're all flesh and blood. Even giants fall. We were bound by the same stories. Read the same works. What greater bond was there between men than to read each other's works? Shultish read Bar-Nun. Bar-Nun read Shultish. The tears on his cheeks, in his mouth. Shultish heard a thud, then clods of earth falling. Now half the link was broken. When was the last time he had tasted tears? If giants fell, what hope was there for normal men? He'd be able to read Bar-Nun, but now Bar-Nun would no longer read him. He could have lived longer. Why not till ninety-nine? He was a man with an infinite number of stories to tell. I know you don't like music or musical imagery, but forgive me, *Adon* Bar-Nun, I can't help thinking along these lines. Your stories were like notes in various combinations. And now the secret of these notes is lost.

Shultish could not see for the thickness of the crowd, but he could hear. He could sense. He could hear a goat bleating faintly on the other side of the valley. A bee buzzing yards away. Crickets in the clover between the graves. Close his eyes and he could see himself on a solitary picnic in some quiet field. Someone— Gershoni?—breathing heavily, irregularly. Then Shultish heard a familiar voice, the cadence of an experienced orator. He did not catch the President's first words, heard only the sonorous, solemn tones, then paid attention to the keen analysis of the writer's life and productivity, his love of the land, his links to it, his many friendships here and all over the world.

"Yehiel, *yedidi"*—the President evidently turned to the grave—"you are gone from us, but you leave behind, as King Solomon said, a good name in everlasting literary deeds. For wherever the Children of Israel are and whenever they turn to the books of the People of Israel, there will be the name and the books of Yehiel Bar-Nun. I know that among you, distinguished friends, writers, colleagues, and translators, there are those who would also wish to eulogize the memory of this great man. We all at this moment carry his eulogy in our hearts. But we cannot hear all those who would have wished to speak. And so, to represent the writers gathered here, I will now call upon a man who knew Bar-Nun many years and admired him—"

Ah, that floating again, Shultish thought. That magical feeling. That ecstatic sensation of bliss. That feeling one gets only in childhood; or when he had Miriam before him, having touched her and knowing he could have kissed her. Levitating in the air. What joy! To deliver the Bar-Nun eulogy. Shultish threw his head back, propelled himself in the sea of air, and floated over the heads of the mourners, soon to land near the President, the Prime Minister, members of the diplomatic corps, army officers, the Chief Rabbis of Israel, the Minister of Culture and Education. What should I accent? ran through his mind. His humanity. His creativity. Jewishness. He hoped his mind would not blank out as it had that eighth day of Hanuka which for Gershoni and his shiksa was Christmas. Which of my works do you like? the sly old dog asks while Shultish's eyes, soul, are mesmerized by that little tree which grew and grew in his mind until it stained his skull green.

"Bar-Nun was a Jew first." The words ring out over the slope of the Mount of Olives. "True, he lived in Israel. But he would have been the same, would have written no differently, had he lived anywhere in the Diaspora." No, that's not true, Shultish quickly thinks. It was Israel that made him what he was. "A man whose entire life and literary creativity centered—"

What?

Lumkin extricated himself from the crowd and, white hair flowing, made his way to the graveside. Lumkin, whom Bar-Nun disparaged endlessly as a hack, a bootlicker, a lacktalent, a sycophant, a literary lackey who arranged literary prizes by wheeling and dealing. Another triumph for a *makher* in the mindless establishment; the old arranger had scored another coup.

Shultish moved his neck several degrees, saw another world.

The hill sloped downward. Seeing was better than hearing. The view of the Old City was magnificent. Who needed Lumkin's words? A great gift stood before him. The Old City walls. The golden Dome of the Rock. El Aqsa Mosque. Between them, unseen, the Wall.

"Here's a story about Bar-Nun that is typical."

Shultish's eyes clouded for a moment; his ears caught the words "story." He focused on the speaker.

"One Purim, Bar-Nun was returning to his house, walking along

162

the Carmel section to a bus stop. He had visited a friend. A sudden downpour began, one of those rainstorms we occasionally have in the month of Adar. A couple, looking out the window and seeing an old man soaking wet, ran down and invited him in. Since it was Purim, they offered him the traditional *shalakh-manot.* Cakes. A glass of wine. They did not know who their visitor was until they asked his name. One year passes. The merry festival of Purim comes again. The family hears a knock on the door. A masked man enters carrying a paper bag. 'Happy Purim,' he cries, and removes a bottle of wine and some cakes from the bag. 'Who are you?' the people shout. The man removes his mask and says, 'Thank you.' '*Adon* Bar-Nun,' the people said. 'You remembered?' 'What a question!' he said.''

Lumkin paused. Shultish said to himself: Only Lumkin can mix mourning and Purim, that *pay-tsadik,* that shmuck.

''Such was the man, remembering a deed of kindness and repaying it with his own surprise a year later.''

Shultish looked past the graves to the Old City again. Bar-Nun was a good man, my teachers and colleagues. A man who wrote as he lived; lived as he wrote. His house on top of Carmel was not only a house. His dwelling on the heights symbolized his own heights as a man and writer. We shall never see such a genius again. With Bar-Nun the tradition of the religious Hebrew writer that begins with Moses ends. My God, Shultish thought. He's the last one. There's no one else who knows the entire tradition. Abraham wore a hat. Rabbi Akiva wore a hat. Yehuda Halevi wore a hat. Bar-Nun too. The last of the line. And who are his successors? Chaps like Gad Nuri or Lev Huri, with no respect for anyone. He remembered sitting at a reception in the President's house, and while Zalman Shazar was talking, Huri—who was scheduled to speak—sat there yawning and picking his nose, obviously sucking the attention of the audience to himself and displaying his impatience, his boredom, his contempt for all to see. Shultish had had to restrain himself from getting up and slapping the man's face. Bar-Nun was the last of the traditional writers, the last one who combined Hebrew and Jewish. The last Jewish writer in Israel.

Shultish looked for Gershoni, found his bare head. "All the rest are your disciples now. You've won, Father Time."

Shultish wiped away a tear.

He felt a tap on the shoulder. Someone whispered into his ear: "Lumkin's drivel makes you cry?"

Shultish turned and saw Lichtenstein.

"Too bad it gives that impression. I turned Lumkin off before he began. I didn't hear a word except the Purim story."

"That's Lumkin for you." Lichtenstein's eyes danced; his chest heaved as he tried to control the laughter. "At a funeral he brings up Purim. At Purim he probably discusses Tisha B'Av and the destruction of the Temple."

"And you think I listened to that shmendrink? I was recalling Bar-Nun with my own eulogy."

"A noble thing," Lichtenstein said. "A very noble thing indeed."

Shultish recognized the red-haired woman and her husband, Moshe, Bar-Nun's son, the one who looked like the Bar-Nun of three decades ago. Another man whom Shultish didn't know was reciting the Kaddish. He was tall and mustached, with a gentle stoop, as though it had developed from his continually bending down to talk to people. Bar-Nun's other son, Shultish realized. The Ambassador to Switzerland. But he resembled his mother; his face had the tiny features of Mrs. Bar-Nun. The burial was over. The crowd was moving toward the Bar-Nun family. Shultish made his way through the crowd. The younger members of the family looked polite. Most of the mourners were Bar-Nun's friends, Shultish noticed, not theirs. The young Mrs. Bar-Nun did not know Shultish. In her husband's eyes a light sparked for a moment, like a falling star, as if he knew who Shultish was. Shultish had never before met the man; perhaps since he now looked as his father had thirty years ago, he recognized Shultish from that half-picture, its memory passed down from father to son, to be awakened when he turned fifty. If the son, now fifty, were reliving his father's life, he should at this point have met Shultish and recognized him. But

Bar-Nun's son was unknown at fifty, so how could he be reliving his father's life? At fifty Moshe Bar-Nun looked older, more careworn than his father. But his mother, Bar-Nun's widow, recognized Shultish:

"How are you, *Adon* Shultish?"

"What can one say, *Gveret* Bar-Nun? *From this grave he'll see the Mediterranean he loved so well.* Of course you and your family most of all, but we all feel we've lost a member of the family. *The Dead Sea is behind us. Dead.* How can words express the feelings in our heart? Our words are so empty. We are not Bar-Nuns. May the Almighty grant you consolation, and spare you further sorrow for years to come." Then in his ribs Shultish felt the elbows of those who were waiting. Waiting to say the same things, he thought.

The Ambassador, who had been speaking to someone, now bent down to his mother. "Mother, did I hear you say, *Adon* Shultish?"

"Yes, Avraham. This is Professor Shultish."

"Ah, Professor Shultish. You are the one I was supposed to give a greeting to. Forgive me for the delay."

"It's not. . . . Of course . . . Then you spoke to my wife?"

"Yes. She called to offer her sympathy. She knew you would be here, and I promised to let you know that your sister-in-law is much improved."

"Thank you. Thank you very much."

Shultish pressed Mrs. Bar-Nun's hand. "No further sorrow." She bit her lips. Her children were at her side. She acknowledged Shultish's words by lowering her head. Shultish stepped back. The wind shifted, bringing the taste of evening, drying the tears on his face. It came from the East. From the Dead Sea. Full of salt and phosphates. The sea breeze of Jerusalem. Shultish turned, looking for the sea. A mile down the road, toward Mount Scopus, one could see the tongue of the Dead Sea licking the Jordan Valley. The Dead Sea. Dead. Not I, he said. I did not kill him, Shultish said.

He heard the sudden silence. Crickets chirped again, heavily. Was it evening already? They chirped so loud only at night. Here it was broad daylight and they were making night song already.

Mir-iam, Mir-iam, they chirped, surrounding him with sound and night. The horizon was a band of crickets. They girded him with sound, like the cloth belt that binds the Torah scroll. In the dead of night where Joshua's sun—the sun he had once held in his hand—was shining on the sea known as Dead.

Another elbow in his back; another elbow in his ribs. These people, even at a funeral, did not practice common courtesy. He had to move on. He walked with the crowd to the buses. Wherever he looked there was a writer of Israel. God, his tape recorder! He could have recorded for posterity half a dozen of Hebrew literature's shining lights. Whom should he seek out first? One could never tell. Perhaps with a good word here, a fortuitous meeting. . . . Lord, Lumkin is walking beside me. He leaned forward, tapped his shoulder. Lumkin, his white hair radiant, beamed and shook his hand. "Memorable," Shultish whispered. "Stirring. As one who has written a book on Bar-Nun I can say you certainly captured—" But Lumkin was pulled away.

Everyone boarded buses labeled "To the Jerusalem Railroad Station." Again the Old City gleamed to Shultish's left. On his right, despite the haze, he caught a glimpse of the Dead Sea. Red-mauve patches moved in the dry heat. The Judean desert shimmered in the heat, hills and rocks and canyons. Shultish's eyelids fluttered. Dry rocks. Jagged colors changed places, refracting the dry background. Finished. Done. Gone. Dead. The Sea of Dead. No more phone calls to him. From him. He'd no longer go through that intricate ballet with a grace of its own to set up an appointment with Bar-Nun. That formal, sly dance of acceptance and rejection. The shifting times. Shifting dunes. Rishon. Miriam. The Bar-Nun library on the desolate clay-colored plain. A picture of a picture of it in his mind. A Fifth Avenue bookstore window. The books of Bar-Nun, translated by Ezra Shultish. And, in a forlorn Hebrew bookstore on the East Side, Shultish's own book on Bar-Nun, on dusty shelves. Look how God spins the wheel of fortune, he thought. Ezra Shultish wanted immortality by translating Bar-Nun, but he ended up writing about him instead.

Shultish stood. Looked about the bus. Gutman was not on it. It would have been nice to talk with Gutman today and reminisce about Bar-Nun, keeping his memory alive on the day of his interment. Recall his words. Discuss something he wrote. Two friends in harmonious recall could with will make a person live again.

The Yemenite girl rose, clambered up the dune, and said, "Father." The slap echoed in the air, clear and stark, resounding over the force of the waves. The water lapped the stones. I stood, faced the old man, and introduced myself, standing next to him, as I had stood next to him at Sinai. Unafraid, not cowed by his power or his wealth, but strengthened . . .

Now that Bar-Nun was buried, the mood in the train changed. That morning no one had spoken of anything but the man; now that he was gone everyone speculated about his literary legacy. A dozen conversations about Bar-Nun's writings were being conducted simultaneously. If Shultish had been able to split himself into pieces, he could have attended spontaneous seminars on Bar-Nun's manuscripts, his relationships with publishers, his early Yiddish fiction, the projected definitive edition of his collected works. Shultish did not know where to turn. Sitting on the arm of an aisle seat, he tuned himself like a radio in and out of several conversations, switching, not knowing where to stop, until he heard a Yiddish writer whom he knew casually in New York.

"People supposedly know Bar-Nun's stories and know the man. Everyone is an expert on him. But the upshot is that they don't know him and they don't know his stories. All he did was put his friends in his stories. No more and no less. Well, I shouldn't say friends, but people he knew and had some sort of grudge against. Everyone he had a grudge against ended up on the printed page."

This made Shultish cry out, "Incredible! I don't believe it. Not Bar-Nun!"

Four people looked up at Shultish, expecting more. Shultish was confused. "He's not the sort," he added.

"Oh, really?" the Yiddish writer continued. "Do you know Asher Mendelsohn?"

"Of course," Shultish said. "He writes for the New York Yiddish daily, *Dos Vort.*"

"Right. He's been writing about Bar-Nun for more than thirty years. And he still doesn't know that he himself is Galili in *Near the Edge of the Town.*"

Shultish jumped up. "Galili—Mendelsohn?"

"That's right." The Yiddish writer folded his arms across his chest.

"Oh, my God, I never thought of that. Reading about Galili I had a sort of familiar feeling."

"Still, Mendelsohn calls himself a critic. Mendelsohn is a critic like I'm a cat. As critical as he is, he can't see beyond his nose, even if the page he's reading shines like a mirror."

A surge of elation went through Shultish, akin to the spurt in one's mind a split second before a joke is cracked.

"You write for *Di Velt?*" Shultish asked.

"So?"

"And Mendelsohn writes for *Dos Vort.*"

"Yes?"

"And maybe it's rivalry talking?"

"Don't be a child! You should hear what people on his own paper say about him."

"What do they say?"

The Yiddish writer grimaced. "How should I know? I wouldn't talk to those *pay-tsadiks* for a million dollars. *Dos Vort,* what a bunch of writers! *Very* talented!"

Shultish turned away for a moment and saw

"Shultish, here you are. I've been looking for you."

Lichtenstein. Shultish clapped him on the shoulder.

"Sit down. Here. This is my seat by the window. I was just sitting on the arm rest to hear better."

Some people Shultish did not recognize—probably those not from the funeral—squeezed to the right to make room for the two men.

"*Adon* Shultish, I'm so glad I could finally meet you." Lichtenstein coughed into his hand. "I wanted to talk about something you wrote."

"With pleasure," Shultish said, ready to talk about his book.

"About your translation of 'The Yemenite Girl.' "

" 'The Yemenite Girl'?"

"Yes. Why so puzzled?"

"Because my translation wasn't published," Shultish said.

Lichtenstein smiled, a wise smile, a cat smile. His gold-capped tooth gleamed.

"I thought you collected only Bar-Nun's published work."

"But, *Adon* Shultish, your translation was mimeographed."

"For a class of ten. It wasn't published at all."

"Oh yes," Lichtenstein contradicted, still smiling, his small eyes dancing triumphantly. "Anything issued publicly, in more than one copy and to be read by more than one person, is considered published."

"How did you get it?" Shultish asked. "It was really something private."

"Everything published about or by Bar-Nun I get hold of." Behind his gold-rimmed glasses Lichtenstein looked briefly into Shultish's eyes and then gazed down, as if trying to hide something. "I'm a Bar-Nun collector."

Shultish looked out the window. The question rode in his mind, skimmed over the rocks and wild grass outside. He brought it in to the sill; his fingers toyed with it.

"Tell me—did you like my translation?"

"That's what I would like to talk to you about."

Shultish's heart fluttered. His index finger trembled once on the sill. He pressed it to the glass to still the vibration.

"Generally it's very good, but—" Lichtenstein hesitated.

Shultish was sorry he had begun the whole thing. To get involved with a pedant, and a collector at that! Crazy as bird watchers, all of them.

"But what?"

"Well, I wouldn't have mentioned that aspect of it on my own, but since you did ask, you'll excuse me for pointing out some things?"

"Of course, of course," Shultish said quickly. "What a question!"

"You did capture the spirit of Bar-Nun's prose, even his rhythms."

Shultish's heart floated higher; he had misjudged Lichtenstein and his intent after all. "Thank you."

"It really should have been published."

"But you just said that anything—"

"You know what I mean." Lichtenstein winked with both eyes. "For a wider audience. It would have been interesting to them."

"Why, thank you very much. Coming from a connoisseur like you, that's really a compliment. You prefer it over Kaften's version in *The Flame?*"

"I have that anthology too. But there are a couple of things in your translation that puzzle me." His glasses glinted once, then twice as he turned his head.

"Do you remember them by heart? I don't have my copy with me."

"I think so. I'm a typesetter, you know. I read a lot and I've sharpened my mind. I can remember pages upon pages, much like the Talmud scholars of old. In any case, toward the end of the first chapter there's a line: 'All souls had met in Sinai; all Jews melt in Israel; and now I was meeting the Yemenite girl.' How does"— Lichtenstein said the next phrase in English—"the word 'melt' fit in there? Bar-Nun repeats the word 'meet' three times."

Shultish felt his jacket sticking to the back of the seat.

"I couldn't have said 'melt.' I distinctly remember translating 'meet.' I too remember. I don't have a bad memory either, and I consider myself a meticulous translator. It must have been a typographical error. The typist may have misread my chicken scrawl. Like Bar-Nun's wife with his handwriting, only my wife can make out my handwriting. A slightly larger 'e' could have been misread as an 'l.' But it's really so many years ago."

"There even may be another one or two," Lichtenstein said carefully.

170

"No doubt, no doubt," Shultish said, not really knowing whether he meant it sarcastically or not.

Lichtenstein listened patiently and nodded. "I can see how a word like that could have prompted a typographical error. After all, I would be the last person in the world to criticize one for printing mistakes."

"Didn't Bar-Nun himself accuse you on the broadcast of making some typographical errors?"

"Well, first of all, he didn't accuse me on the broadcast. Only I spoke during the interview, you will recall. It was I who related the anecdote. But you're right. Of course! I've been guilty of that too, occasionally. But there is something else. If I recall correctly, in the first chapter, when Bar-Nun talks about life on the beach and its rhythms, there's a line that reads, in your translation, 'My rhythms are slower.' Something to that effect. I'm not familiar with that line in Bar-Nun's story. Is there a version in your possession that I don't know of? Some periodical that I've missed, perhaps? I have all his variants, you know, from first newspaper printing to short-story anthology, through the three editions of his collected works. But there are very few variants of this story. Perhaps you have another, one I'm not familar with, which has 'my rhythms are slower.' If you do, I'd be grateful if you'd tell me where it is. The fact is, I just don't remember that line."

Shultish did not know whether he blushed. He thought he did. His shirt was stuck to his jacket. His insides were sweating. Even the rocks outside, in the unsettled wilderness alongside the tracks, were sweating too. A peculiar white ooze, perhaps from birds or reptiles.

"I don't really remember the text offhand," Shultish said, "although I should, because I like that little story."

"Well," Lichtenstein said, looking somewhat aloof, as if he'd been caught associating with someone who was his intellectual inferior, "you didn't just simply add those words, did you?"

"I may have bracketed them—to explain them to my students. It was done for them."

Lichtenstein looked around. Others who had attended the funeral were gathered in little groups. From time to time the name

Bar-Nun was repeated, like a chant. It surfaced again and again, with a rhythm, a litany all its own.

"If you'll excuse me, *Adon* Shultish, you seem to have done this a couple of other times—"

Shultish was yearning to look at his watch to see how soon they would arrive at Ramle, where Lichtenstein would have to get off and change for the Tel Aviv train. But he didn't want to give the impression that he wanted to be rid of the man. He was sorry that he had gotten into the conversation. Every man pursued his own glory, looking to aggrandize himself at the expense of others. Shultish glanced out the window. Perhaps he could tell by the scenery how far he was from Ramle. They were just leaving the Judean hills; the countryside was spinning, a flat, horizoned disc in motion.

"And when he talks about the different types of knowing, where the dimensions increase from one to two to three, you add, 'depending on the depths of the people.' And another phrase in the same paragraph, 'a game of two-part harmony.' Bar-Nun would never have used a phrase like that. That's a metaphor from music. In all his works there is no such image."

"Those are my notes." Shultish raised his voice. "Explications."

"But they're not bracketed."

"It wasn't for publication. It's a private matter. One cannot, one dare not, review an unpublished work. I didn't send this version to you as an editor for consideration. Or to any critic for his criticism." Shultish pushed his hand behind his back; he felt his fingers shaking, his face flaming.

"I'm not a critic," Lichtenstein said.

"With that I agree one hundred percent. You're not a critic. But you're a dispenser of criticism. You're taking a translation that I made privately and are making public examination and trial of it. You're putting me through a cross-examination, a third degree, as if I were a criminal."

"One should not tamper with an author's text."

"I didn't tamper with it."

172

"Then I don't know what else to call it. Especially if its tension is reduced by gratuitous additions by a man who would like to rewrite a master's story."

Two little men were pounding on the sides of Shultish's head; another worked on his abdomen, sucking air out of it. He looked at his watch; the numbers were juggled around. He looked for the three, found it wandering between seven and nine. Eight sliced in half, just a shadow of its former image.

"You're just a typesetter, *Adon* Lichtenstein. And a frustrated critic, who probably never even dreamed that politics plays a role in Bar-Nun's works. Don't look so surprised. You've been typesetting creative artists for so long that you think you're writing their works. Meanwhile you're only copying. There is a difference between copying and creating, *Adon* Lichtenstein. There are those who create and those who copy. There are those who create and those who *collect* creations because they can only copy. You print and print and print. But you don't publish. I don't recall ever having seen anything with your by-line in print, *Adon* Lichtenstein."

Shultish was ready to rise, to excuse himself and go to the men's room, to bring an end to the conversation. His jacket was now part of the seat. He was certain that a foul odor of sweat—his—like a horse's, was pervading the car.

"Guilt speaks from your mouth, *Adon* Shultish," Lichtenstein said, rising. "Otherwise you would not abuse me in this fashion. A man should be creative in his own stories, not in other people's works. . . . Excuse me," Lichtenstein said. He rose, went to the men's room, slammed and locked the door.

Shultish walked to the next car and sought the toilet. He felt a pressure on his bladder but could not urinate. In response to some older politesse, he flushed anyway so that no one would think he was just wasting his time there, or doing other things—like Gershoni, who had the Christmas tree in his house replanted in Shultish's skull. He checked the door; it was locked. No one could come in. The metal bolt was slipped over the latch. I know things about Bar-Nun that you'll never know. His views on Langweil. His views on who is safe. His views on Hebrew literature. Go on collecting. Collect shadows, fantasies, the tails of clouds.

The train was moving. He opened the window and looked out. Even during the argument the earth had spun beneath them. He saw boulders and trees flying by in the foreground, revolving as though on some moving stage near the horizon. The Ramle station must be near. Good riddance. He'd have it easier to Haifa. Soon the sun would set. There was a dampness in the air that had not been present in Jerusalem, where the air was dry and cool. The entire sky was above him, a band of colors like a rainbow. The sky promised peace and tranquillity after the annoyance of Lichtenstein. The colors were in the key of blue, as if in a twelve-tone scale ranging from mauve to purple to deepest navy. He could not see the line between one color and the next, but if he let his eye sweep over the sky, he could distinguish one band from another. On the horizon several ridges of hills twined. Maybe nature was truer than literature, after all. It didn't have so many phony pedants and egoists working with it. The hills looked like dolphins, or playful mermaids, caught in midleap in the air. Two lines of telephone wires crossed his vision. They reminded him of the double lines in children's Hebrew notebooks between which the letters should be placed. Two birds perched on the wires. The dots on unseen letters *shin*—the initial letter of the word shmuck. Which Lichtenstein, now departing at the Ramle station, definitely was.

. . . by my love. I stood and faced the powerful old man who considered my pale skin and my culture inferior to his, despite the fact that we both had stood at Sinai and were of one color then, neither as light as I nor as dark as he. I stood at the top of the dune, looking at him, seeing him framed by shoreline and sea.

Shultish sat on his veranda looking out at the Mediterranean. It presented its plumage like a bird, its colors and textures like a woman. The weather reminded him of late May, when trees are fully green. The April chartreuse bud and translucent leaf had disappeared. The season seemed old, in full leaf. Old and secure. Time had suddenly slowed down, immobile now in the sunny days of June.

Now that Bar-Nun was dead he was gradually becoming a void in Shultish's mind. Although Shultish no longer had the urgent desire to see the old writer, nevertheless, one morning as he was walking along Herzl Street carrying half a liter of milk, he thought he saw Bar-Nun strolling up the street ahead of him. The same rounded shoulders, the old-fashioned broad-brimmed hat. Phantasmagoria. Should he follow? What nonsense! It couldn't be he. Yet suppose it was, and Shultish missed the opportunity. If the ghost were greeted, he might return gradually, and Shultish would be playing his role in a destined game. He quickened his pace and watched the man's back, but as in a Chagall painting, he saw Bar-Nun's face while looking at his back. He passed the man, closed his eyes, opened them, looked to the right, slowed down, and turned.

Shultish's own story was progressing slowly. Now that he had the tape, he had no great desire to see Miriam. Now that he had the tape, he had no great desire to hear it. So Bar-Nun had been right after all. Shultish looked out to sea, floating on a raft. Reading and relaxed. The air was cool. His thoughts moved like stars in the galaxies, distant, silent, aloof. Without effort. He knew his story well; he saw it before he fell asleep, those magic moments when he would weave Persian carpets and compose symphonies. He had not written a story for so long he had thought he no longer knew how. Still, what he had written pleased him. Maybe something had rubbed off after all—the contact with Bar-Nun and all the other writers.

The day his wife was to fly home from Switzerland, Shultish woke early. She would be home by two in the afternoon. The birds' singing was heavy in the trees. Every leaf had a bird. Did the trees flutter because of the trilling of the birds? Did their song shake the leaves and cause a breeze? They didn't all sing at once. Those at the top began and their song continued clockwise; it made an O shape on the tree. Shultish looked at the calendar. It was the thirtieth day after Bar-Nun's passing. Time to hear his voice again. As a tribute, a memorial to the old man, he put on the tape of "The Yemenite Girl."

What went through my mind then? What did not go through my mind then? I pictured many things. I pictured myself at my writing desk at the slab of flat stone on the jetty, composing various alternatives that were washed away by the sea, as a sponge washes chalk from slate.

When I thought of the sea, I thought of life. And yet thinking of the sea reminded me of futility; for eternity the waves kept rushing toward the shore, but all in vain; the five or six meters they gained in the morning they lost that afternoon. Yet the waves and wavelets maintained their stubborn attempt to storm the shore.

The Yemenite girl rose, clambered up the dune, and said, "Father." The slap echoed in the air, clear and stark, resounding over the force of the waves. The water lapped the stones. I stood, faced the old man, and introduced myself, standing next to him, as I had stood next to him at Sinai. Unafraid, not cowed by his power or his wealth, but strengthened by my love. I stood and faced the powerful old man who considered my pale skin and my culture inferior to his, despite the fact that we both had stood at Sinai and were of one color then, neither as light as I nor as dark as he. I stood at the top of the dune, looking at him, seeing him framed by shoreline and sea.

The sea rushed forward, washing everything away. Her father looked at me as if he were gazing beyond me. The Yemenite girl rose from the sand quickly and whispered, "My father cannot see very well." She took my hand and walked to the sea, where the shadows were deeper, until the water swirled about our feet louder and louder and a chorus of mermaids chanted and wove their seaweed song in rhythms the like of which man has never heard or felt. We were both encompassed by the arms of the sea, which long as they are can never touch the tops of the dunes, where the sea never comes and mermaids never sing.

It was Friday. The Sabbath Eve mood already hovered over the city. Even at seven in the morning Shultish heard the splash of water on tiled verandas and the sound of rag mops. The air was cooler, wetter. Bar-Nun might have said that on the eve of the Sabbath the Lord was bringing up a fine mist from the Mediterranean to cool the city. Rugs were being beaten. Yemenite and Moroccan girls—like duplicate copies of a photograph—were scattered on various balconies on various floors beating Persian and Bokharan and Caucasian rugs with bamboo beaters. Aromas of baking floated in the air like currents. Challahs and poppyseed cakes and chocolate yeast cakes like those his grandmother had made in Russia were being delivered in bulging baskets. It smelled like Friday. It tasted like Friday. Even with his eyes closed and ears stopped up, he would have known it was Friday in Haifa. Peace filled the air. Screams subsided. On a day like this the Messiah would come. The tranquillity of the sea, of a quartet—*pace* Bar-Nun—by Haydn. He walked to his room. The bay spun by, the trees, the streets. The hills of Haifa revolved with him. The whole world was in motion again, propelled by his walk. In Eastern Europe it was the husband who returned to his wife on Friday after his business journeys; with Shultish, his wife was returning to him.

The phone rang.

"*Shalom,* Shultish. Gutman here. Have you read today's *Ha-et?*"

"Not yet."

"Read it."

"I usually do. Anything special?"

"Yes."

"Aha. Don't tell me. I know what it is."

Gutman paused. "Has anyone called you yet?"

"No. But I know."

"All right. Let's hear it."

177

"A tribute to Bar-Nun for the thirtieth day after his death."

"You're psychic."

"Not really. I just have a calendar. And I reason well. Ratiocinative, if you know what I mean. Read Poe. It's not hard to guess that *Ha-et* should have the traditional tribute today. Who wrote it?" Shultish swallowed. A sudden spray of jealousy brought bile to his throat. "You, or Lumkin?"

Gutman laughed. "No. . . . You know who did? Bar-Nun!"

"A tribute to himself?"

"Again no. A story."

"Really? A posthumous story? How wonderful, Gutman. What good news you've brought me. And I was just talking to him."

"What?"

"I mean he was talking to me."

"Shultish. You're starting again. I said psychic. Maybe psychotic, God forbid! Shultish, you're acting abnormal again. Are you all right?"

"Of course. I was just playing my tape. My own tribute. . . . Is the story good?"

"Good? What a question—and from you. His finest. Real and symbolic."

"What's it about?"

"What's what about?"

He's exasperating me again, Shultish thought. No wonder Bar-Nun couldn't stand him. "The story, of course. What else were we talking about?"

"Well, I think you ought to read it yourself. It's on the literary page."

"Thanks for calling, Gutman."

His Friday was perfection. What heights of harmony, then, could his Sabbath aspire to? Shoshana returning and a Bar-Nun tale. He went out on the balcony again, pressed his hands on the railing and looked out at the sea. Saw toylike boats bobbing in the water. Took a deep breath. The cool air entered with its Sabbath aromas. And a story by Bar-Nun for the tranquillity of Sabbath.

Shultish ran out to buy the paper. He sat on the balcony,

scanned the headlines first to keep himself in suspense, then opened to the literary page. Saw title and by-line. At first the letters joined to form words, and his eyes skimmed over the lines, unable to convey meaning to his mind. The words sang individually but made no sense collectively. In his excitement to read the story he rushed along, feeling like a lad who has eaten too much too quickly. He reread the lines, put words together until they formed sentences. Read the sentences until they formed paragraphs and plot. This time the words made no sense; he was not aware of them. Like watching pictures passing, he saw the scenes, unhampered by words. Then it struck him. From afar. A blow between the eyes. His head spun as though the virus had returned. The sour feeling in the abdomen came next, and he fully realized what he was reading.

On this thirtieth day after Bar-Nun's death, on a Friday morning which bore the tranquillity of the Sabbath, Shultish was reading a story by his friend Bar-Nun. About a British professor of Hebrew literature, a writer from London who had pretensions to being a translator and critic of a famous Hebrew writer's works; a man who always sought to be near him, and unconsciously assumed the older writer's walk, ways, style, and speech patterns.

At first Shultish covered himself with the paper, so that it formed a little tent over his head. He'd never be able to face any Hebrew writer in the world again. He was finished. Marked. Stigmatized from the grave. He gazed at the Mediterranean, absorbing its blueness, its calm. Then, slowly, as slowly as the freighter making its way out to sea, as slowly as the blue speck on his lips turned from salt to sky, second thoughts surfaced. He had been too hasty. Many of the things that Bar-Nun had said were not true. First of all, he was not from London. Second, Shultish has not aped Bar-Nun at all. Third, Shultish was fifty, Bar-Nun's character fifty-eight. He was of medium height, rather stocky; Bar-Nun's hero tall and thin. It was fiction, fact decorated with plenty of imagination. Shultish lifted the paper from his head and looked around. No one was staring at him. From the balconies no fingers were being pointed at him.

He began to read again. Gutman was right. The story was a masterpiece. And he was the central character. Even if slightly changed. Modern literature needed masterpieces. And heroes as well. A vacuum that had to be filled.

He looked out to sea again, the sea that Bar-Nun had loved so much, the blue sea that were Bar-Nun alive both of them would now be gazing at. Two different sets of eyes directed at the same sea that gave so much pleasure. The sea in which he and Miriam and the Yemenite girl, all the Yemenite girls, had bathed. The sea stretched out like a blue silk curtain, so tight that the children playing down there, like dots beneath Hebrew letters, could jump on it like on a trampoline.

Bar-Nun and I, he thought as he dozed off—he's given me a gift that can never be taken away. Still, they could have set it on the first page. After all, Bar-Nun's first posthumous work. In the distance he heard the sea as clearly as if its waves were touching his veranda. Saw the mermaids in the undercurrent, playing with the piers, their metallic voices glinting to the green sounds of the sea. Higher and higher, and louder and louder, until the arms of the sea, sight and sound, encompassed him, in the mountain where the sea never comes and mermaids never sing.

He blinked, eyes open, the sea stage before him. He felt like dancing. A mad tarantelle on it. The story, he remembered, as he floated on a raft of clouds. He and Bar-Nun. United. In print. Forever. Paper and pen. Hand in hand. The picture completed now.

Known.

Immortalized.

THE YEMENITE GIRL
by Yehiel Bar-Nun

Translated from the Hebrew
by
Ezra Shultish

א

I saw the Yemenite girl sun bathing by the sand dunes of Rishon. Not in San'a, not in Haifa or Hebron, but in Rishon I met her. I was not afraid of her because she was swarthy, for the sun had honey-hued her skin. On the contrary, I found myself drawn to her hair, fragrant as wine, and to her eyes that shone gently, like the water at dusk off Rishon, when the westering sun sends blue light waving to Jerusalem.

I saw her first from the sand dunes as I sat by the green dune grass. She sat at the foot of the hill, where the white sand was so soft that the foot sank in deep with each step, and one felt like a primordial creature slogging languidly through the mud, lifting one leg and then another, on the way to the sea. She played with the sand, letting it run through her fingers as sand runs through an hourglass. She watched the rilling white sand; I watched her sun-tanned fingers. I saw her nostrils, curved and chiseled in perfection—that cut of pride and daring—and then her well-formed mouth and eyes that spoke an ancient language I under-stood so well. But I did not stop there, for one's eyes become intoxicated with a beautiful thing, desiring more. From looking at her face and fingers, I looked at her hands. From looking at her hands, I moved to her arms and shoulders and body. As I gazed at

181

her I thought of honey, the honey and milk that is the essence of Israel.

Every day the Yemenite girl bathed in the sand, the sun, the sea. I too came daily, for there is nothing in the world like the sand of Rishon and the water of the Mediterranean, which is cool even on the hottest day. He who has not bathed in the blue waves off the dunes of Rishon has never bathed in beauty.

I don't know what the Yemenite girl did. I don't know whether she worked and came only after work; or whether she was not employed at all. Perhaps she was a rich merchant's daughter and had the time to loll by the sea, or perhaps she was a poor cobbler's child who could find no employment and, to compensate for her sorrow, came to bathe in a water that soothes all sorrow. I don't know what the Yemenite girl did; what I did, I know.

After work I would come to the sea to let my body and my spirit relax. I walked on my heels on the damp sand licked by the tide and watched the little white halos that disappeared as soon as they were formed. Even on a day when I ceased work early and came at eleven, she would be there too. Perhaps it was coincidence that we shared our hours, but then again perhaps her hours of work were as odd as mine.

I am not the sort who pushes himself on others; born in Nicolsburg, I share my forefathers' values of propriety and grace. When asked if I am kin to the famous Hasid, Reb Shmelke of Nicolsburg, I lower my head and do not deny it. I say this not out of vanity, but out of loyalty to my saintly ancestor and to my town. For cities, like families, have a character, and they lend to its sons the things they learn. And so, because I stem from Nicolsburg, I did not rush to her; I did not preen like a peacock and come to conquer. I have seen friendships quickly formed and quickly broken. I know life on the beach; I know its rhythms; its rhythms are as alluring and powerful as the unending rush and ebb of water to shore. My rhythms are slower and, I hope, longer lasting.

I knew the Yemenite girl long before I knew her. I do not play with words, or with paradoxes. There are three levels of knowing:

the outer—of dress and mannerisms, the way the hair is combed, a person's walk and gestures, the shape of his face when he is tranquil or angry; but all this is one-dimensional, seen from the outside, observed from afar, while the observer may still be a stranger. The second level of knowing is the one in which the observer also becomes observed, in which every word and gesture becomes question and answer, a game of two-part harmony. Here the dimensions increase from one to two or even three, depending on the depths of the people. The third kind of knowing is the most mysterious and intimate of all, when man knows woman, Adam Eve, in a net of ecstasy.

Reticent and shy by nature, I took my time in getting to know the Yemenite girl. First, because I thought I was destined to know her. Second, because she was always there, or almost always there. Only once did I feel her absence, when I sought the sea breeze one afternoon. I climbed the dune by the path-no-path I always used, looked down and saw empty space and sand in the place where she always sat. Seeing sand and emptiness, I thought of the desert. In the distance I thought I saw something strange: the figure of a young camel. But the sand is deceptive, in desert and shore. What I thought to be a young camel straightened and stood; a man with a knapsack had been tying his shoes.

Then I remembered the Yemenite girl. At that moment, when my heart felt empty too, I realized that I knew her better than I thought. How can one miss a person one doesn't know? How can one find one's heart empty if the person hasn't filled some part of it? Hence the reverse must be true: I must have known her: she must have already filled some part of my heart. And if I did know her, from where did I know her? We surely did not work together; we had no friends in common. There were no other places I could remember where we might have met. But then I realized I had erred. There was a place where we had met. The place where all of us had gathered, the souls of Jews born and unborn, all present at the Revelation. What matter, then, that she had made her way through the desert and settled in Yemen and that I had trekked to

183

Europe? All souls had met in Sinai; all Jews melt in Israel; and now I was meeting the Yemenite girl, whom I had gotten to know best the moment she wasn't there.

ב

I used the flat rocks of the sea as my writing table and considered how I could approach her. I thought of this and that, and all the thoughts turned to water and slipped through my fingers. But I did not just go up to her. I got to know her the following way. Occasionally I would nod to her and she would smile back. We could have remained just nodding acquaintances, as I am with the man down the street whom I greet daily but if not for the mailbox on his gate would not even know his name. Then the simplest thing occurred. She went to bathe and returned shining wet, like a mermaid emerged from the sea; but then, as I was going to the water, just as our paths crossed, she stumbled. The Lord had placed a stumbling block in her way for me. She stumbled, and I rose.

ג

Some days later I learned that she indeed was a rich merchant's daughter, even though Yemenites are not usually merchants. That her father was rich I had gathered, for when she told me her family name I immediately recognized it; it was known in Israel, just as my kinsman's name was known in Europe. When I asked her if I might come to her house that evening, she shook her head and said, "My father."

ד

Those words made me want her all the more. Not only did I have to win her love, I also had to vanquish the father and his pride. Why had she said no to a visit to her home? Did her father not allow her to go out? Could it be because my skin was not

184

honey and the whites of my eyes not milk? Would white skin like mine be anathema to him? My origins too lowly? A man like me, descended from noted Hasidim and men of valor, not good enough for his daughter because I came from Ashkenaz and he from Yemen? Had we not stood together side by side at Sinai? Had we not, together, heard the sound of the shofar increasing in strength from moment to moment? Had we not, together, heard the thunder, the mountaintops clashing, seen the sparks of lightning made by stone grating stone and absorbed the words spoken at the Revelation?

ה

I saw the Yemenite girl in the evenings. Not at her home or at the sidewalk café, but by the dunes I met her. In honor of our meeting, the tide withdrew and gave us room, sand and space more than we needed. She clung to me with fury, not thinking of her father. But her father, transparent as film, came between our embrace and made me think of him. Her embrace told me that she thought of now; mine tried to keep from her my thoughts of what would be.

Although the water kept a respectful distance, it still roared and rumbled. The sky turned the color of ripe plums. Sea gulls cried and dived for fish. The sun had set and left its afterglow on the horizon, as if the Holy One Blessed Be He had smeared the dying red sun along the length of the sky. The world was at peace.

"Your father," I said.

"No," she said softly. "Let us not talk about my father."

I looked into her eyes. Sometimes her eyes were blue, sometimes brown. They shifted colors, as the dunes shifted their shape. Isn't it odd that something you own you cannot see—until someone else comes along to provide the light?

"And you?" I said.

Her eyes looked into mine and gave them light to see. "I have my own mind—can't you see?" she said.

"What would your father say if he knew?"

Yemenite girls are gentle and gracious. But mine, in addition,

185

had a resolute mind. "We will not talk about my father now. He is of a different generation." And then she gestured to sand and sea. "But I was born here."

"And hasn't he already chosen a husband for you?"

The Yemenite girl did not reply. Was it the question that made her blush and become even more beautiful at that moment, or was it the truth behind the question? She laughed silently. Scoffing at whom? Or what? The question or me? A husband has been chosen for her, I decided. But her kisses belied that thought and chased that suspicion. Her lips were sweet; honey was under her tongue; the fire of Yemen was in her heart and her love.

ן

On the land, by the sea, under twilight and sky, when pomegranates and columns of marble seared our thoughts, we postponed the words that harbor deep in one's soul and which we fear will surface.

The questions gnaw, like Scorpio, and never cease until they triumph.

"You'll have to come away with me, as Ruth followed Naomi."

"One can become a Jew," she said, laughing, "but one cannot become a Yemenite. An impossible conversion."

"Then you'll convert." I laughed in turn. "You'll come away with me."

"And leave my father?"

"And woman shall cleave unto her husband and leave her mother and her father," I quoted.

We sat side by side, hunched into the sand, our hands hugging our knees, as if excluding others by that self-embrace.

Then a shadow crossed our line of vision.

"My father," she said.

The shadow approached, fell over the dunes.

186

What went through my mind then? What did not go through my mind then? I pictured many things. I pictured myself at my writing desk at the slab of flat stone on the jetty, composing various alternatives that were washed away by the sea, as a sponge washes chalk from slate.

When I thought of the sea, I thought of life. And yet thinking of the sea reminded me of futility; for eternity the waves kept rushing toward the shore, but all in vain, the five or six meters they gained in the morning they lost that afternoon. Yet the waves and wavelets maintained their stubborn attempt to storm the shore.

The Yemenite girl rose, clambered up the dune, and said, "Father." The slap echoed in the air, clear and stark, resounding over the force of the waves. The water lapped the stones. I stood, faced the old man, and introduced myself, standing next to him, as I had stood next to him at Sinai. Unafraid, not cowed by his power or his wealth, but strengthened by my love. I stood and faced the powerful old man who considered my pale skin and my culture inferior to his, despite the fact that we both had stood at Sinai and were of one color then, neither as light as I nor as dark as he. I stood at the top of the dune, looking at him, seeing him framed by shoreline and sea.

The sea rushed forward, washing everything away. Her father looked at me as if he were gazing beyond me. The Yemenite girl rose from the sand quickly and whispered, "My father cannot see very well." She took my hand and walked to the sea, where the shadows were deeper, until the water swirled about our feet louder and louder and a chorus of mermaids chanted and wove their seaweed song in rhythms the like of which man has never heard or felt. We were both encompassed by the arms of the sea, which long as they are can never touch the tops of the dunes, where the sea never comes and mermaids never sing.

Temple Israel

Minneapolis, Minnesota

In Honor of the Bar Mitzvah of
JEFFREY MALMON
by His Parents
Mr. & Mrs. Al Malmon

December 30, 1978